HELP
FIRST

Sell Less,
Profit More.

CHRIS COOPER 2015

Prologue

You depend on your business, but you hate selling.

This is the biggest pain point of the entrepreneur. And this book will solve that problem.

Ten percent of readers will only need the first chapter of this book.

After reading, "What do people WANT?" you'll have the big "Aha!" moment, rethink your service and marketing, and run with the ball.

That's what this book is about: helping people best. Finding what type of help your clients need, and how much, and when.

When your clients know they need your help, you'll never have to sell anything again.

This book is organized like an inverted triangle: the big idea first, then general strategies, and then very specific tactics. Keep reading until you can take action; don't stop at the first epiphany. An idea without action is just a wish. Wishing doesn't help anyone. But helping your clients will benefit you both.

What Do People Want?

This is the question every gym owner, every accountant, every hairdresser should ask.

No matter the industry, you're in the helping business. And like most people, you probably hate selling. The very thought of asking someone for money—ugh. But it's gotta be done, right?

"How do I get more people to pay me?" is the wrong question. But it's the one most people ask me.

My name is Chris Cooper, and I consult with professionals who want to make more money. I don't sell anything, but I help hundreds of people. And I'm rewarded financially for it.

The difference between helping and selling comes down to one word: intent. If I want to help you get what you want, I'm not selling. If I'm trying to get only what I want, I AM selling.

Ironically, the best salespeople in the world know this fact. "You can have anything you want in life, if you just help enough other people get what they want" is a famous Zig Ziglar quote. But Ziglar is usually introduced as "The World's Greatest Salesman," not "The World's Greatest Helper." If you can figure out what people want, and then provide it, you'll be successful.

So what DO people want?

The answer lies outside of any sales textbook or University marketing course. The answer starts with a brief introduction to human psychology, as illustrated in Maslow's Hierarchy of Needs:

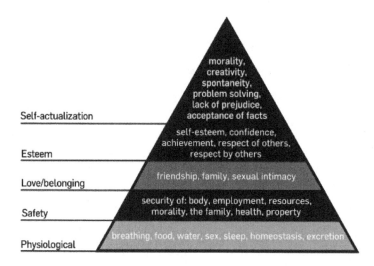

The base of Maslow's pyramid is security. Humans don't have shells, and we're not prickly to the touch. What gives us security? The tribe. Being part of a group. Fitting in. Even better: becoming a celebrated member of the tribe instead of the outcast left for the lions. Moving up Maslow's hierarchy, people want LOVE. They want FRIENDS. Obviously, there's an overlap with our need for security, but more than the security of the tribe, people want to feel like they're part of something. I'll talk about ways to help people become part of a movement later.

Maslow's next level is Esteem: people want to have self-confidence, and that means being successful often enough to believe in themselves. We'll talk about "Frequenting the Podium" and other ways to boost Esteem later in this book.

Finally, self-actualization. In my 2012 book, "Two-Brain Business," I asked readers to describe their "perfect day." I've collected over a thousand responses now, and found a big surprise: NONE said they'd stop working permanently. Nowhere was the "sit on a beach for the rest of my life" answer I anticipated. No one even said they'd like to win the lottery. Being "self-actualized" has little to do with wealth or free time. So what does self-actualization mean?

For most of us, it means doing something important to others. It means the right level of eustress--the good type of challenge--to keep us engaged. It means finding problems and identifying a path to solutions. It means finding an exciting learning curve, not finding a saggy beach chair.

Thanks to Maslow, we know what people want most: security. When they have security, they want a relationship. When they have a relationship, they want esteem. And then they want an optimal level of challenge.

You can provide ALL these things.

Look at your customer with new eyes: are they really visiting you because their hair is getting too long, or because they need your help impressing a date? Will your service help them charm their future wife?

Are they visiting your gym because they want to "look good nekkid" or because they're embarrassed to be seen on the beach without a t-shirt? Do they really just want to "firm up a little," or are they worried their wife no longer finds them attractive?

You're not selling these folks anything. You're simply providing the help to overcome a huge rock in the road.

The "Help First" strategy might require you to look at your business with new eyes. It might be challenging if, like me, you've been in the service industry for a LONG time. But asking, "How can I help?" will do more than improve your marketing: it will improve your life.

Knowing that I plan to spend the day helping people makes it pretty easy to get up at 4am every day. Having a PURPOSE is necessary for success.

The right level of guidance is also necessary. For example, some readers of this book will want a roadmap: "Just tell me what to do, say and charge for it!" There are templates toward the end, but none will work without purpose. Others readers won't want to fit their business into a mold, and that's fine; learn the concepts in the next few chapters, and apply them in to your purpose.

When I was fifteen, I was shipped – with a small group of other "gifted" kids – to France and England for a whirlwind tour spanning a total of about 10 days. We were met at the airport by a guide; shown to our bus; dropped at our hotel; met by the guide in the morning; taken to lunch by the guide…for ten days. Our days were scripted down to the last statue, from the wakeup call to curfew. There were a few very short periods of exploration on our own, and of course, those are the times I recall best: getting served beer in a pub; following a monk through his island monastery; jumping to see over the sea of heads surrounding the Mona Lisa at the Louvre.

A few years later, I went to Australia for a month. Our vacation included a rental house and car…and no itinerary. We saw a bit of the coast, spent a day walking around Old Sydney Town, and checked off the typical Touristy things…but also spent many days watching television in our rental. Without a clear plan, we stagnated. Sure, we climbed the Blue Mountains, and had a few other highlights, but the time between those was…well, *wasted*.

Just as different readers will seek different levels of instruction from this book, your clients want different degrees of "help." After reading, you'll understand how to keep people engaged by letting them choose, prioritize, and play with your service.

Guided choice means more help, more engagement and more retention for your clients. Creating a map, as you'll see, will allow a client to choose how much guidance they want. Some clients want to explore your services over time; others will want step-by-step guidance.

For the business owner, Maslow's Hierarchy IS our map. The first step to selling is to understand how to help. Explaining how your service provides help at each level of the Hierarchy is marketing. Selling means being a tour guide.

What do YOU Want?

Understanding your own motivation is key to helping others. Your clients' goals and desires are very likely to reflect your own, so we'll start there.

The first exercise my consulting clients are assigned is called "Perfect Day."

Here's the "perfect day" exercise in a nutshell:

One year from today, if everything is going perfectly, what time do you wake up in the morning?

Do you go to work? At what time? What do you do when you're there?

What time do you come home? Do you work weekends?

How much vacation time do you take?

Finally, what kind of income would pay for those things?

Interestingly, after posing this question to thousands of gym owners, no one has ever said they'd quit work. Most said they'd sleep in, or take more vacation, but NONE said, "I'd retire."

After the exercise, most realize money isn't the goal; money is a tool to help them reach their goal. Your clients have goals, too; and they have money.

When you have a goal, you have a "Point B.
"The next step is to figure out "Point A": where
are you starting from? What advantages do
you have? Who fits in your audience? Who is
already there? Why did they find you? How do
they benefit from your help?
We'll discuss these in great depth later.

What do WE Want Together?

One of the greatest lessons I hope you'll pull
from this book is to see your service through
your client's eyes. Think about what THEY
want, not what YOU would want in their shoes.
Here's an example:

When we bring a new gym into our consulting
practice, we usually recommend they add
Personal Training as an option for new clients.
Often the gym owner will reply, "That's way too
expensive. No one's going to pay for it!"

And, of course, many WILL pay for it. Personal
training is a fantastic value for higher-income

folks: a flexible schedule, no wasted brainpower, and efficient use of time. But until I became one of those high-earners myself, I didn't understand the value of time. We extend our belief system and values onto the people we meet; it's a natural phenomenon.

And it's a trap for business owners.

The first way you can help your clients is to tell them what they need instead of what you think they can afford.

If you own a gym (like I do,) people come in the door to be coached, not sold. So coach them: tell them what to do based on what's best for them, not what's cheapest for them.

If you sell dresses, sell the dress that will make her look great...not the dress that's on sale.

If you're an accountant, set them up for long-term success; don't just try for the biggest tax return.

The "Help First" strategy can get you to your "Perfect Day." And a "Perfect Night's Sleep" means an easy conscience. Don't short-change your clients by giving them anything other than what's best for them.

What DON'T People want?

In other words, what do people want to AVOID?

Creating desire for a service is the focus of modern-day marketing. But as smart marketers know, showing people how to avoid what they DON'T want can be even more powerful.

This could mean highlighting a clear and present danger: "Don't swim here! Sharks!" Or it could mean leveraging what people fear most—public embarrassment—and providing a solution. On the other end of the spectrum, it could mean creating a "problem" and then solving it.

For example, Gatorade has largely created the "sports drink market," and then amplified the fear of dehydration with the Gatorade Sports Science Institute.

People are afraid of imminent danger, and tend to underappreciate long-term risk. Many will clutch their wallet tightly in a dark alley, but fail to make contributions to a retirement savings plan. It's human nature: we fear the shark attack, though we're far more likely to be killed by heart disease.

Deodorants and toothpaste aren't desirable on their own, but avoiding the fear of social repulsion has made them billions. As I wrote in Two-Brain Business, emotion drives action. You can tell a person what to do, but until they have an emotional reason to take action, they usually won't.

As different strategies and tactics are revealed in this book, it's important to remember both the focal point of your message and the consequence for ignoring the same. This is especially true when trying to help groups of people make the right choices.

Who is our client?

A year ago, I posted a topic on a popular online message board titled, "What Can A Great Gym Do…That It Doesn't Yet?" I offered a free Catalyst Gym t-shirt to the best idea. Some great stuff came forward, and I was extremely proud that we were already doing 90% of the good ideas. The t-shirt went to a user named "sumabeast" for his idea: a "study lounge:" couches, tables, and some textbooks. Would this be a great idea for a big GloboGym? No way. A library in a gym is square footage that isn't driving revenue. It wouldn't appeal to a membership interested in burning calories instead of reading. In fact, this doesn't fit the fast-food-fitness model of compartmentalization and "No Loitering" at all! That made it a great idea for MY gym. A couple of dorm-room-style couches, some free coffee, and some textbooks lying around made a fertile seed bed for growing my gym community. My client at Catalyst is interested in intellectual pursuits as well as physical exercise.

This "gathering place" concept isn't unique to gyms, of course, but gym owners looking for a way to distinguish their service can benefit more than most. As the functional fitness industry explodes, so does the perception of our service as a commodity.

Malcolm Gladwell talks about the inverted-U of attention in his book, "David and Goliath." Gladwell writes most about the back of the hump: when a force is so large that it actually creates its own weakness. In the case of Goliath, he argues, the 'giant' was so large and ungainly that a nimble rock-hurler could crack his head without being caught and trampled.

A big gym chain can't pivot to meet the needs of every individual client—but I can. And the big guys don't like it.

Am I taking a thousand clients away from the neighborhood treadmill factory? No. But hundreds of thousands of exercisers are now moving away from pec-decks and elliptical trainers. They want barbells and gymnastics rings, and the big chains don't have any.

Their only defense is the sticky (but mostly false) story about safety: they'd like my clients to believe that my gym will injure them. That story appeals to people who are scared of change (i.e. almost everyone.) These are the folks who see the CrossFit Games on television, and their fears are confirmed: they can't do this. It's too hard!

They'll never be at the level of Annie Thorisdottir. They believe they have to 'get in shape' before trying our workouts. Or worse: that everything we teach is out of reach, including basic barbell exercises and handstands.

These are the people who need me most.

I need to change their minds not through rational head-on argument, or repetition, because that will only make them MORE resistant to our service. Instead, we need to change their minds a tiny bit at a time.

As I wrote a few years ago, trains can't take a sharp corner. You have to create a slow curve, a gradual transition to your point of view. You need access to them. To give them a hand up, you may need to take a step down to their level first.

Several gyms in my Mentoring program now offer a low-pressure version of box programs: a 'boot camp,' 'Intro to CrossFit' or 'Lite' program. If the barbell scares a client, take away the barbell until they're not scared of the gym anymore. If they're worried about getting "too bulky," show them they won't by allowing them to try METCON-only classes. Let them avoid your Secret Smolov progression until they believe they're ready to step up into programs at the box.

Some gym owners, under the pretense of "purity," will be appalled by this idea. To them, I ask: what is our responsibility? It's the long-term progress from sickness to wellness to fitness of our clients. If it takes a Zumba class to get Aunt Bess to see these outstanding programs in your gym, will you do it?

In the end, what other business owners see when we look at our business doesn't matter.

What the CLIENT sees is what matters. Show them a picture they like.

Over time, their views will shift to your perspective. Don't rush a potential client into something they don't want; instead, try to keep them around for 20 years and lead them slowly.

The bottom line: you are not your client.

In a few pages, I'll introduce a method for identifying who your client REALLY is; what THEY want; and how you can help.

Target Markets

People use your service for a variety of reasons. It's important to know what benefits they want to receive.

No one gets a haircut just because they like to sit still under a rubber apron. No one hires an accountant just to make an expensive friend who shares a love for math. When people seek your service, they're really seeking a benefit.

Harvard marketing Professor Theodore Levitt: "People don't want to buy a quarter-inch drill. They want a quarter-inch hole." They want to hang their picture. They don't want to know about titanium alloys or any of the other features; they just care if the tool can provide the benefit.

Mary is getting her nails done because she wants them to match her dress. Tom is going to the gym because he has a new girlfriend. Sally is getting her taxes done because she's scared of an audit.

Knowing the benefit your clients are seeking can guide our message. In fact, forget about the services you offer for a moment, and think about the benefits your clients are seeking. Do they want a clean car for the parade? A six-pack for the beach? A table near the window to impress a date? A pain-free lower back?

Then build your services to address those benefits. In other words, solve those problems. Fill those "wants."

If we segregate your audience by the benefit they're seeking, we can call each one of those small groups a "target market." Using one of my businesses as an example, here's a list of target markets for gyms:

Fat Loss

Sports Performance

Job Performance (fire/police/military)

Kids

Pain Relief

Rehabilitation

Obstacle Course Race Prep

CrossFit athletes

Corporate (happier workplace)

Instead of breaking down your markets by demographic information like age, use desired benefits. The solution for fat loss differs by degree, not kind, for a 20-year-old and an 80-

year-old. But not every 20-year-old wants the same thing.

Each of these is a separate target market. How do we help those who want to lose fat? The optimal answer should be your primary service. The optimal question is, "What will BEST help this person?" instead of "What's the cheapest / fastest / newest way to help this person?"

When a teenaged girl comes in to get her hair done before Prom, she wants you to ask about her dress. If you can match her dress to a shade of nail polish, you're helping her; the cost will be a secondary consideration.

When her mother complains about the cost of prom, it's okay to mention the dress shop that offers 20% off to your clients. That's helping mom AND the dress shop, and they'll likely return the favor (more on that later.)

Every new client carries a problem to be solved. Solving the problem is your job.

Understanding the problem and presenting a tailored solution will make you a great business. How do we know what our future clients want?

I know where you're going after work.
In the words of every stalker, "I'm not a stalker." But your behavior is predictable. And so is mine.
Each of us spends most of our time in one of three places: at home, at work or the "third place" -- a hobby, a church or a sport. This third place might be different for you than for me, but doesn't generally change. We're creatures of habit.
According to Ray Oldenburg in "The Good Great Place," the third place is necessary for creative interaction (hobbies or sport,) and usually has its share of regulars. Thousands of years ago, villagers left their tents and hunting grounds to meet at the campfire and engage in dance or storytelling; today, we snap shut our MacBooks and meet at Starbucks. Or the gym.

We influence the people at those places, and they influence us. When your friend recommends the Sumatra blend, you'll try it. Otherwise you won't. Our influence is moderately strong among our friends, a bit stronger at work, and strongest at home. And since we don't have much influence anywhere else, you're most likely to share opinions in the same fashion.

Marketing is leveraging influence.

Old-timey marketing relied on mass broadcast for influence. Television ad people talked about the "trust factor" of their news anchormen; newspapers were written at a sixth-grade level to appeal to the most susceptible market for their sales. But no matter how strong Palmolive's message, a 1950s housewife would still choose PearlWhite dish soap if that's what her friend recommended.

Advertising no longer works. We're immune. We won't be fooled again. And yet...we need to trust someone. We need to belong, to demonstrate our sameness, to reserve our spot at the campfire. So we duplicate the tendencies and habits of those around us to "fit in." If that tendency is to use Palmolive, we'll do it.

I know you work in the service industry (that was an easy one.) You're not selling dish soap, or any other commodity: you're selling your time, and that's an exhaustible resource. Spending your time wisely is important. Wasting time on "advertising" or other marketing gimmicks is a missed opportunity. Some of the strategies in later chapters will require a small time investment, but they're a no-lose proposition. Talking more with clients, and offering to help in creative ways is never a waste of time. In the best case, you gain a new client or help an existing client find a higher-value service. But even in the worst-case, you've helped someone. It's the exact opposite of most "sales" practices, which leave you feeling guilty or anxious when the sale is made. When you help first, you feel better no matter what the outcome.

As I tell my kids, "The purpose of life is to make other people happy." Helping doesn't feel like selling to you—or to the potential client.

Time invested in knowing your audience will recoup a massive dividend. Ask where they work, and about their job. Ask where they go after work, and what their husband does on the weekends. Take a genuine interest. Don't pay for ads; pay attention.

As you'll read, relationships—not transactions—are the foundation of success.

The Client Continuum

Further confounding the problem of "What Do People Want?" is that humans change our minds often. The answer can change depending on time of day, hunger or fatigue; on what they've recently read; and especially on what their friends are doing.

However, trend data reveals consumers falling into four broad categories, depending on when they use your service:

1. Early Adopters
2. Early Majority

3. Late Majority

4. Laggards.

Each group above desires a different outcome from your service. Though the service might not change between groups, the benefit sought by the potential client DOES shift. The first step to knowing, "What do people want?" is to identify their motivations over time.

Early Adopters

The Early Adopters are the risk-takers. They're explorers of service; they want the new iPhone before anyone else has one. Motivated by novelty and being on the cutting-edge, the Early Adopters will use your service because it's new. But this isn't the whole story.

These "first on the bandwagon" clients are usually prequalified: they'll come into your salon carrying a picture of a hairdo they like, or into your CrossFit gym with an "Infidel" shirt on. They know their stuff, and will push their authority.

The Early Adopter is REALLY motivated by renown. He might want the new iPhone for its features, but he really wants everyone else to know he got it first. He wants to WIN, in other words, especially if he gets a podium.

"Dude--is that the new iPhone 12? You got it ALREADY!? Wow!"

Because the Early Adopter likes to talk about "winning" the race to have the product first, they can spread the word quickly. Usually, they're enthusiastic, because saying "this new phone sucks!" is a conversation-ender that won't feed the conversation. They're your first Mavens, in other words.

Early Adopters can be convinced with logic or emotion. They're drawn to new points of view for the sake of difference. Make a good case for your service, and they'll emphatically back it.

Aside from recognition, Early Adopters can be swayed with extra features. The "Star Wars" series has been packaged and repackaged many times to include upgraded behind-the-scenes footage, deleted scenes and other junk only a "true fan" would have. We can help the

Early Adopter find your service--especially if it's new--with a tactic called "Founder's Club."

The Early Majority

The second group of patrons are eager for novelty, but aren't quite as brave. They'll wait for Consumer Reports to tell them about the new Google glasses, or their foodie friends to recommend that new restaurant. They want to be hip, but they also want assurance: they don't want to take big social or financial risks. Usually recruited by the Early Adopters, the Early Majority is motivated by change. Many will be using a competing service (they're already having their hair done elsewhere, but decide to try a change.) They likely won't make a large financial jump (going from a $100 phone to a $1000 phone) or huge social jump (they might try your gym if their friend is already there, or their mom goes to a similar gym in another town.) The Early Majority is mostly swayed by social proof: if they read stories about people like themselves enjoying your service, they might try it. They need to know the risk has been mitigated; that others have jumped the gap.

Later in this book, you'll read about Mavens Strategy and individual invitations. These are both particularly effective with the Early Majority clients (but work with everyone else, too.)

The Early Majority client is usually more influenced by social pressure than by authority or expertise. Where the Early Adopter is prequalified and pre-sold, this second wave is less educated. They'll want to know what your service can do for them, or how you'll solve their problem. While the first purchasers of the Toyota Prius fell in love with the concept (and mileage,) the Early Majority client wanted to know how much money they could save over the lifespan of the car. They waited for rebates or recalls. But they didn't buy another car in the meantime. In other words, they were paying close attention while the car proved or disproved its value. When Early Adopters nodded their approval, the Early Majority jumped aboard.

Late Majority

This group is late to the party, but the party is still going strong. Their testimonial story will start like this:

"I finally got up the nerve to try..."

These are the more reluctant late-joiners on the tail end of fashion. They require more social proof, more authority and more work to start, but are also more likely to stick around long-term. They don't need novelty, but DO need to feel special. They don't change habits often (or easily,) and tend to set down roots. Their reluctance is offset by their loyalty. Interestingly, though more cagey about trying a new service, the Late Majority client has had time to do their homework. They've likely considered all the angles--and probably "almost joined" a few times. They've probably driven past your office more than once without coming in. But they also know your service inside and out (or think they do.) This is the danger: the Late Majority is often "late" because they're paralyzed by too much information.

The Late Majority client will try to impress with knowledge; this can come across as arguing. Maybe they've read some different opinions on hiring employees versus hiring subcontractors, and want to gauge the strength of your opinion. They're NOT making an appointment to schedule an argument, but can frustrate you in a first meeting.

Keep this in mind: the long-term value of a Late Majority client is usually more than any other group, because when they believe in you, they'll keep believing forever.

Laggards

These folks are out of fashion; they're not 'hip.' They discover your service after everyone else has already moved on to something else. We're all laggards in some areas: my teen clients roll their eyes when I refer to "the Instagram." We do likewise with our parents' political convictions.

Laggards will visit your bookstore after you've sold the last copy of the new Grisham novel. They'll ask for that cool hairstyle from "Friends." They'll complain when you change the menu.

The best thing you can offer a Laggard is advice. Not all-at-once, in-your-face "get WITH it, man!" advice, but a slow change of course. "Why don't we try it THIS way today?" or, "You can still do it exactly the same...with one small difference. Try it, and you can always go back..."

Obstacles To Helping

(And How to Overcome Them.)

Lack of Context

Zig Ziglar, "America's motivator," tells the story of himself as a young pots-and-pans salesman. Driving the red-dust back roads of rural Georgia, he once knocked on doors for several days in a row without a sale. He was getting desperate; with a wife to feed at home, he was burning gas and getting lean. Finally, one family – likely too polite to turn him away – let him into their living room. Now, in rural Georgia in the 1950s, there wasn't much entertainment, and Zig put on the show of his life. They passed around his non-stick pots. They nodded at the time Mama would save washing dishes. They agreed that Mama shouldn't be burning her hands three times a day--but they couldn't afford the pots. They had no money, they said, but thanks for taking all that time. "Here, Mr. Ziglar, have a little cookie before you go...." They brought out a beautiful china plate, heaping with cookies. Ziglar remarked on the beauty of the china, and mentioned that he'd only seen that particular pattern once before: in a catalog he carried around with his pots. The family grew excited, and asked him to show them the catalog. He did. They ordered a set worth two hundred dollars – a TON of money in the 1950s. As he was writing up the deal, curiosity got the better of him, and he asked, "How is it that you didn't have money for pots, but you can afford fine china?" Mama smiled. "We don't have money for pots. But I've been saving for fine china for years."

The first obstacle to helping is the perception of value. Your perception of value is determined by your background, your history and your urgency.

Stop: before you go any further, remember that your client's sense of value is not the same as your own. A huge mistake made by many service professionals is to project their own sense of "value" onto their clients.

Context makes a massive difference.

In the service industry, as with plates and pans, the value and the price are rarely the same.

In the fitness industry, the value of exercise is the avoidance of a heart attack; it's a longer lifespan; it's joy. If the client lacks this perspective, he won't know what to ask. So his default question will be about price.

"How much is personal training at your gym?" he'll say. The client has no other criteria on which to compare your gym with another.

You can try to objectify the value of your service. "Well, a heart attack costs $110,000." Or, more commonly, "We don't know why Bill's Gym charges $300 per month, but we're cheaper." A better approach is to teach the value of what you're providing.

Since the proof can't be objective, we'll use the psychological phenomenon of social proof. Social proof occurs every time a consumer looks to friends, peers, and assumed experts for recommendations. This is where Facebook shines: athlete biographies, expertise essays, member photos, tags, shares, and the ever-important like button are all valuable tools to creating context. Pictures of your members, hung in your box or posted on your website and Facebook page, are also a great help. Mentions of their friends' successes reinforce the love of your current members.

Leading the conversation away from price, and toward value, also makes for a smoother signup process for both you and your clients. Asking potential clients about their Bright Spots-- what they envision a healthy, fit body will mean for them--shows you are invested in their success. When an overweight client comes in for a consultation, we ask for the things they're doing right, NOT the things they have to change. Then, when we ask them to think about the first indications of success, they gain perspective on our rates. Asking, "How will we know we're being successful?" invites the client to try on success like a pair of pants. Rather than mentally balancing their checkbooks, they can imagine looser clothing. They can balance the value – weight loss –

against the price – our rates – rather than merely comparing numbers against numbers. In the case of my own Mentoring program, I like to ask new entrepreneurs to identify Future Bright Spots: things that will indicate success. "I'll be able to sleep in!" say many, or "I won't worry about how I'm going to make payroll on the 30th." Those are things I can deliver. If the conversation centered on price, some business owners would have trouble putting the rate into context. However, by demonstrating value (more sleep, more peace, more money,) most are eager to be coached.

In your own business, talking about value during the first conversation will help steer the relationship in the right direction. Consistently delivering value will keep the conversation away from price. When a client asks herself, "Is this worth the money?" you're not delivering on your social contract.

I'll cover the intake and discussion process in a few chapters.

Misperception of Value

In the summer of 2010, gas prices in North America spiked. They rose quickly – by as much as 7c per liter (or 27c per gallon) in a single day, eventually shattering old gasoline price records.

Outraged, the public demanded blood. Public inquiries were held. Politicians made phone calls. Gas companies blamed the New Orleans refineries, which blamed the price of crude oil. Public officials who suggested a cut in the taxes levied on every gallon were shushed. Slowly, the price dropped back to the new 'normal' – about 80c per gallon higher than before the hike. They would never drop all the way back.

By late 2012, gas prices again reached the tip of the 2010 spike. They rose slowly this time, by 2 or 3 cents, every few weeks. Consumers watched it happen, and took no action. No outrage, no politicians, no discussion this time. Why?

The trick is a popular one, well known in the business world. By exposing the consumer to a price that's far out of line with their expectations, a marketer can alter the price that a consumer EXPECTS to pay.

In your brain, you create "anchor" points to help you quickly estimate values. For instance, if you're going out to buy a dozen eggs, and you have $5, you don't stop at the bank machine; you know that a dozen eggs costs between two and four dollars. That's your price anchor for 12 eggs. When you order a beer at dinner, you estimate that a domestic draft will cost between three and five dollars; you don't have to ask the price. That's your price anchor for beer.

When CrossFit gyms began to appear across North America, they didn't have a value problem; they had a price anchor problem. The public didn't have a mental category for an Affiliate gym, so they compared rates for box coaching to gym memberships. I encouraged box gyms to compare themselves to Personal Training prices (and still do.)

Increasingly, the public is becoming aware that box programs are not typical gyms. Now that future members have an "anchor," pricing can be set accordingly:

1. First, a high-end, all-in rate. This will be the option taken by about 20% of your prospective members; it exists to provide the service to the minority who can afford it, but more importantly will set the price anchor high, making the next offer appear more affordable in context.

2. Your REAL rate. The best training you can provide at a price that will let you live the way you want to live.

3. A bargain basement 'cheapie' rate that might allow people to test the waters a bit, like a one-week pass.

Another solution is to use a stratified structure: an unlimited membership with a below-average price, and several additional options for clients to choose from. The Stratified Model for gyms is covered extensively in Two-Brain Business 2.0.

Your Ego

Stop telling your athletes, "You're doing it wrong."

"Stop being late. Stop choosing the wrong weights. Stop talking when I'm talking. Stop leaving your stuff behind. Stop cherry picking."

Instead, tell them why in advance.

"The warm-up is important because…."

"The goal of 'Grace' is to spend 4-7 minutes in an anaerobic zone. Choose a weight that will let you finish 30 cleans and jerks in 4-7 minutes."

Say things that are important.

Thank them when they do things correctly.

Tell them that the workout is hard, and that's the point, in advance. Not after; before.

Good teachers, good parents, and good coaches know this. Life gets easier when you do.

You Hate Selling

Professional salesmen occasionally say they have a "two-hundred-pound phone." They mean, of course, that sometimes it's hard to pick up the phone and try to make a sale. Even after decades of selling, they sometimes dread their job. Sales is possibly the only career you can despise even as you improve.

No one hates the sale, really. But everyone hates social risk. When you ask someone to buy from you, they gain the power in the relationship. You can't MAKE anyone buy; can't steal clients; can't trick anyone. Not anymore. It's always up to them. And your ego is on the line; closing a deal is like asking for a first date. Imagine asking for ten first dates every day!

Now imagine taking your first date to a place they might not enjoy, and then sticking them with the bill. THAT'S how we imagine "selling" must feel, right? Like we're tricking someone, and they'll find us out and expose us for fraud. Selling a product or service is all about YOU: your commission, your quota, your record. That's the problem.

Luckily, we can avoid all of it: the ego, the emotional baggage, the feelings of dishonesty or being "too slick." We don't have to sell our service at all.

Helping someone is all about THEM: their happiness, their progress, and their wealth. If you see a person as a prospect, you can't help them. If you use a sales "technique," they'll resist you (people know when they're being "techniqued.") But caring enough to help always returns far more than the time you invest.

I don't want to sell if I can help it.

Aiming for Transactions, not Relationships

Most also shrink back from "selling" because of the transactional nature of the sales process.

"You want my money? That's all I AM to you!?!" that's the response most service professionals fear. Personal rejection is hard, and we'll do anything to avoid the experience, including dropping our rates. We don't undervalue our service, but we're scared to tell others how we value our time.

Fostering relationships takes longer. Relationships contain many transactions, but don't feel like a "sale" or "process." There's a constant give and take in any successful relationship, but a marriage doesn't end after you've washed the breakfast dishes. In a relationship, there's no scorekeeping.

For example, a happy client doesn't total every transaction with you; they simply attend their Friday appointment and leave happier than when they arrived.

In some cases, a transaction is enough. Lost cat? You don't need to forge a relationship with the finder; you just want your cat back. Police officers don't need long-term relationships with tipsters; they just want to find the burglar. But these are the exceptions, not the rule.

Even commodities like dish soap now realize the value of dating the dishwasher. They try to appeal emotionally, by adding scents or advertising "that feeling" the buyer will get when using their product. Unfortunately, these same companies have been training buyers to shop for the lowest price for decades, and that's a hard habit to break. You can't go back on "we're the cheapest" later. When you attract clients seeking "cheapest," you turn away the clients seeking "better"---and you'll soon lose the "cheaper" clients, too. You can't be cheapest forever; why not be better?

Focusing on a long-term relationship means focusing on "Help First." As Bob Burg wrote in his fantastic book "The Go-Giver," you don't have to be a better "people person; you just have to be a person." This means approaching every person as if you're seeking a new friend instead of a client.

When you want to belong to a circle of friends, whether it's your first day in elementary school or first day in prison, what do you do? You help one of them. You want to fit in, so you're desperate to do the leader a favor. Right? Why not approach every person you meet this way, even if there's no obvious way for them to return the favor?

Starting a relationship means you're not keeping score. You're not scratching a back in hopes of being scratched. You're not looking for "win-win," but just helping THEM win. When your value exceeds your cost, you'll be successful.

One hot summer Saturday, I was circling a residential block in my truck. My wife had successfully bid on some gymnastics mats in an online auction the night before, and I was headed to pick them up. I was a bit skeptical; these mats usually retail for about $400 each, and her winning bid was $102 for two. In my mind, I pictured moldy old worn-down mats covered in bird droppings. I had the money in my pocket, but I was ready to haul both straight to the dump if necessary.

When I finally found the house, the owner didn't answer the door. I thought about packing it in, and started walking back down his drive until I heard a grunt from under the huge RV parked out front. I crouched down beside it and saw the owner working on the axle.

"Hi, I'm here for the mats!" I said. He rolled out without a word and led me to a storage shed. I tried to engage him in conversation, but he was almost mute. He didn't even shake my outstretched hand. But I forgot about his mood when I saw the mats.

Like brand new, two giant gymnasts' mats stood solidly in the middle of his plastic carport.

"They just need a hose-down," he said. And it was barely even true: they looked as if he'd just opened them yesterday. I was curious.

"Do you have a gymnast in the house?" I asked. He toed the dirt and started grumbling.

"We DID," he said. "My daughter is twelve. She took gymnastics at the club down the street. But it was crazy expensive."

I thought the mats--easily worth $800--must have added to the cost, but I held my tongue.

"So you quit?" I asked.

"No, they promoted her to the competitive program. It actually costs less--only about a hundred a month--but it felt like they did it to keep us around longer, you know?" He virtually spat out the words.

"Did she like the competitive program?" I asked.

"No, she hated it. But she felt like she couldn't go back to regular gymnastics classes after that, so she quit in the spring. Now I've got these things." He gestured back to the mats again, and we began to carry them to the waiting truck.

Neither of us said anything until the second mat had been loaded. But then I couldn't help myself: I hate seeing kids stop exercising.

"Listen," I said, "These mats are worth a LOT more than a hundred and two dollars. I know we agreed on that price, but I'd like to help your kid. I run a big kids' program at my gym, and there are a lot of ex-gymnasts there. They do some gymnastics, some running, and some Ninja Warrior stuff. I think she'd probably love it."

Wary of a sales pitch, he literally rolled his eyes at me. He thought I was trying to get my money back.

"Bring your daughter up to try it. If she likes it, I'll give you two months free. OK?"

He looked confused. What else could he ask?

"How much is it regular?"

"Seventy dollars," I said. "But she can come every day for two months, if she likes. No commitments after that."

He brought her two days later. She loved it. She STILL loves it. And as he said to me on Saturday,

"She uses those mats more now than she did when they were in our basement." And he smiled.

Paralysis by Analysis

Many of your future clients are terrified of looking dumb.

They don't want to make the wrong choice because they'll be judged harshly. Their husband will condemn their spendthrift ways. Their friends will make a different choice, leaving them isolated and alone. They'll no longer fit in with the group.

So they dither. They read reviews, weigh pros and cons, and "give it time." They take no action. They need you to move them. The best thing you can do to help someone at the moment of choice is to pull them forward.

First, make choosing simple. In "The Art of Choosing," Shyeena Iyengar published her research on how people choose. It's a long book, but boils down to this: too much choice is overwhelming. Give a new client two or three choices, and they'll choose their favorite. Give them four choices, and they'll choose none.

I recommend three levels of service: a "budget" level, a "regular" level and a "platinum" level. When paying for services, people tend to fall on a Bell curve: about 20% will want the cheapest available option; 60% will want the middle option; and 20% will want the luxury option. We can influence their decision by framing the middle ("regular") service with higher- and lower-priced versions.

What service should a new client choose? Frame it with higher- and lower-value propositions. Most will aim for the middle choice.

For example, if the best way to start a fitness journey is through ten personal training sessions, your offer could look like this:
a) One personal training session - $99
b) Ten personal training sessions - $850
c) Twenty personal training sessions - $1599

Which drew your eye? Likely the middle one. I've written about "price framing" extensively in Two-Brain Business.

Next, always present an "A" and "B" over a "Yes" or "No." Do you want your tires cleaned, or just the rims? If presenting two options instead of three in the above example, it could be framed this way:

"Do you want to try one session now to see if you like it, or set up all ten to get the discount?"

Nowhere is an option to "go think about it." But this isn't a slimy Glengarry Glen Ross "Always Be Closing" technique. You're simply recommending the best service for your client based on your expertise and knowledge of their needs. Then you're removing the Tyranny of Choice, to use Iyengar's phrase. They know they need your service; you know they need your service. Why stop them?

Third, know when to stop selling.

Talking more is never better. Listening is the best way to convince someone (more on that below.) When someone is ready to receive your help, the best thing you can do is get out of your own way.

I started my sales career in a ski shop. Located at the base of a mountain, we stocked a few dozen "demo" skis: the high-performance sets with big price tags. At the end of the season, we'd sell off these demos at a discount.

When the snow started to melt in March, renters of the demo sets would stomp into the rental shop and ask the price of the skis. As a passionate skier (and reluctant salesman,) I'd rave about their choice...and then talk about the other skis they hadn't tried yet:

"Those Rossignols are super fast. Have you tried the Volkls? They're great too, and the turn radius on the Atomics make them feel like racecars. Have you tried them yet?"

Confused by too much choice, the client would usually leave with nothing. I was stopping them from getting the new pair of skis they wanted.

When a client is looking for a house in the East End, you don't extoll the values of the West End. You book a showing in the East End, because that's what THEY want. You might prefer the nightlife of the West End, and wonder at their choice of quiet streets and overpriced lots in the East End. That doesn't matter; what matters is what THEY want. They

want the quiet lots. They want the Rossignols.
Let them buy what they want.

Fourth, lead with questions.

Your job is NOT to teach anyone the difference
between AC motors and DC motors in
treadmills. It's not to show them every treadmill
in the store. It's to ask, "What do you want this
treadmill to give you?" Show them the brand
that will best serve their needs. Then stop.
You're the expert, and experts don't need to
hedge their bets.

Ask if they agree with your choice.

"Based on what you just told me, I think this
treadmill will fit you best. Want to try it?"

"What do you think? Will it help you with your
goal? After using this treadmill for a month,
what results do you think you'll notice?"

"How soon do you want to get started?"

Lead with questions. Let the client make the decisions and lead the conversation. You're just an enabler.

One final consideration: it's very difficult to walk a client UP in price, but it's easy to walk them DOWN. This is a psychological phenomenon called "framing," where the first price sets the context for the transaction.

Think of the last time you bought a car: after spending $35,000 on your SUV, the salesperson asked if you'd like the sunroof option for an additional $300. After spending $35,000, an add-on seems very cheap.

But if the salesperson had started her pitch with the sunroof--"This part costs $300, the seat covers cost $800 and the rest of the truck costs $35,000"--you're less likely to buy any of it. The $35,000 number seems bigger after hearing about the $300 part.

Your value to the client is 100% equivalent to the value you create in their life. Changing their mind without a good reason will only create doubt and buyers' remorse. Let them feel good about their decision. Then reward them with Bright Spots later.

Discounts

The service industry is full of caring people. Good people, who want to help others. Sometimes these good people are tempted to help others who really can't—or won't—pay full price for their service.
My advice: help those who DESERVE it, not just those who NEED it. You'll never run out of the latter.
Our goal is to provide maximum value for the client's money, and receive maximum value for our time. There's a trend among service providers to use discount services--like Groupon, for example--to "get people in the door." It's easy to believe that more clients =

more revenue, whether they're paying $5 or $500 each time they use your service.

Unfortunately, attracting a high number of discounted clients creates a downward spiral. A discount-seeker has prequalified himself as price-sensitive instead of value-sensitive. They're also more likely to be drawn away by the next bright shiny offer, creating a cycle of discount marketing and low retention. In short, companies who routinely discount their services for first-time clients will always be chasing MORE clients and earning less than they should. Their business becomes a revolving door of lower-value clients. Where does it end?

The cognitive error comes from a misunderstanding of the Onboarding process. Many businesses believe Awareness is the problem; that, if people just knew about their excellent service, they'd fly through the door in flocks. But that's usually NOT the problem: desire is the problem. And coupon-cutters desire one thing: to save money. Not better service, but cheaper service.

When the couponers arrive, the professional works hard to maintain a high level of service. After all, the owner is after the long tail: a client who will stick around at normal rates for a long period. In many cases, the pro is willing to sacrifice their time at a very low income in hopes their "investment" will pay off. They're trading their most valuable resource (time) for their least-valuable client.

In the late 1990s, at the same ski resort, I was introduced to a "sales trainer" to learn how to sell ski vacations to large groups. One of his messages stuck: don't spend time on the "maybes."

The clients who immediately accept your help-- the "YES!" clients--are great, of course. But the "NO!" clients aren't bad, either, because their up-front denial allows you to move on to others immediately. Only the "MAYBE!" client can kill you.

The discount-seekers are ALL "maybes."

If Martha is trying your service without a coupon or special rate, she's already done her homework (or can afford to be wrong.) But if she's waiting for a deal, she's a "MAYBE!"--she isn't sure, or can't afford your full rate. To keep her, you'll have to sacrifice either time (providing your service for less than it's worth) or money (you'll have to keep the deals coming to keep her.)

What's the answer? A clear Onboarding plan that addresses all stages of the client relationship.

A "help first" mentality that will allow clients to KNOW the quality of your service before they're faced with a buying decisions.

And an Action plan for your brand, on which you deliver consistently and with excellence every month.

When a client experiences your product at 50% off on her first visit, she'll be forced to ask herself, "Is this worth double the price I'm currently paying?" If you provide the full value for half the price, how will she ever make the mental jump to paying more? And if you provide a lesser service for the lesser price, you'll STILL have to sell up to the full service.

Worst of all, when Bill--a long-term client paying full price--hears about the discount, he'll wonder why he didn't get one. Is the new client more valuable than he?

Maybe, he thinks. Maybe.

Vague Service Offerings

(What's better than free?)

"Our unlimited membership is $200...but includes FREE open gym, FREE personal training, and FREE nutritional advice, plus FREE weightlifting and FREE yoga..."

What's wrong with that?

As Chris Anderson explains in his excellent book, "Free: Future of a Radical Price," North Americans have a funny relationship with "price" and "value."

Unlike the rest of the world, where value is determined through tough negotiation, we ascribe value to things with a high price. We take things with a higher cost more seriously. Anderson points out the power of a single DIME: when you have to pay for something— even if it's only ten cents—you value it more. Gift certificates printed on heavier paper stock carry a higher perceived value than flimsy copier paper. If something is expensive AND limited, its perceived value rises even more. Put an expiration date on that gift certificate, and it's more likely to be redeemed.

In conversations with over 750 gym owners, it's obvious they're trying very hard to create value for their clients.

The owner knows the value of free Open Gym, of free one-on-one coaching after class, and a specialty group on Thursday night because they're giving up something valuable (their time) to provide it. Unfortunately, the client doesn't place the same value on these things. They don't KNOW the value unless they're told.

As an example, consider the problem of no-show clients for free "introductory" sessions. Catalyst doesn't have a problem, and neither do most gyms that charge for OnRamp programs. But gyms that charge a very low price—or do free classes to teach beginners—DO have a problem with clients who don't show up.

A stratified pricing model is attractive because clients know the value of every service they're receiving. If they don't think Open Gym time is worth $40 per month, they don't pay for it. But if they really want to train with the competitors, the $40 per month isn't a problem.

Another example: I give out a LOT of free resources at twobrainbusiness.com, and I'm sometimes asked why our mentoring program is in such high demand. After all, clients COULD just use the free resources and chart their own map.

But the value is in the one-on-one approach, the accountability and the price: they're paying for it, they have an appointment on Tuesday, and so they'll do the work. They take it seriously.

The value of a service is different for everyone. What do your clients value highly? What do they value more than finding the lowest price?

Overcoming Price Objections

Adding revenue streams like Personal Training is obviously a huge benefit to gyms.

But almost every time I mention it to a box owner over the phone, I hear this:

"My market won't pay for that." Substitute the word "demographic" for "market" if you want. This has happened nearly 400 times now. And the problem usually isn't with the client.

The first step to overcoming price objections is to fix the owner's misperceptions about their clientele.

1. Often, a gym owner doesn't believe their members will pay more for one-on-one coaching because the owner wouldn't pay for it themselves. Maybe the owner can't afford it; maybe they don't see the value. That doesn't matter; their clients CAN, DO and WILL. This is called the "false-consensus effect," and it's a cognitive error.

2. Not every member has to switch to Personal Training. If you consider the Bell Curve of client spending habits, you'll see that about 60% of your clients are happy with what they pay for your service. 20% think it should cost less (and will pursue a lower-cost option.) But 20% would pay for more if it were available. These 20% can pull the Bell Curve to the right, increasing the average revenue per client. They're also the most likely to stick around long-term.

3. Not every person in town makes an average wage. I live in a steel town where both major industrial employers have declared bankruptcy

in the last five years. Per capita income has been cut by a third. But that doesn't mean my average revenue has been cut by a third. It doesn't mean everyone is broke.

4. Value is more important than price. In a class of 12 people, a client who is struggling to get her first muscle-up might get ninety seconds of individual coaching. But if she can just nail that transition, she'll love your workouts even more. What will help her more: your divided attention in a group, or 30 minutes of uninterrupted focus, where she can work through a progression, see a video of herself, and be assigned homework to get her to the next stage? To her, this service is worth far more than the $40 a half-hour of PT would cost. In the words of Jeff Lynch, a dentist and owner of CrossFit Alpha 1 Athlete: "Don't try to diagnose someone's wallet. If they don't want the service, they'll say no. But if they want it and you don't tell them it's available, they'll find it elsewhere."

5. Some coaches don't want to "sell" personal training, because they share the same

cognitive bias. But if the same coach is given a chance to do a PT session with you, or another coach, they'll quickly see the value. Then they can talk about it in class, and make recommendations without feeling slimy.

1-on-1 training also offers a point of entry for people who want to try your gym but are intimidated by group classes, or have a "special" condition. It's also the fastest way to improve a client's skill in any lift or gymnastics progression. It's a good way for your staff to create a meaningful career, and is often the best fitness solution for many clients.

Bill, a gym owner, was undecided about one-on-one training until he tried offering it to new clients. He didn't force it on anyone; just added it as an option to his menu, and told people about it. Here's what he thinks now:

"We have been doing our current intro session, with modest success for the last 3+ years. It was not tailored to the prospect's needs, basically gave an overview of our CrossFit classes and some theory/history of CrossFit. I though that was what people need to hear.

Since changing our approach, with the help of Chris, to a goal setting session as an intro, where we discuss the prospects goals and essentially actively listen to the them, we have seen our clients getting a better introduction to the program, feeling more involved in the process, and creating more revenue for us.

I have been amazed at how well this is working for us. Almost everyone will go with the Fast Track through this change alone, we generated about $4,000 extra this month, which is huge for us as that is about 1/3 of our income right there."

Many coaches cut themselves off at the knees by considering what THEY want instead of what their CLIENTS want.

How do you know what your clients want? How do we identify the 20-30% who prefer individual attention to group classes?

1. Ask them.

During our No-Sweat Intro session, we spend most of our time listening. What brought the client to us? What do they want to achieve?

After they've explained what they want, research indicates that clients are likely to sign up, but still want to feel as if they have a choice. Offer them A or B, instead of Yes or No.

Example:"Would you feel more comfortable trying a group class, or would you feel more comfortable learning to train one-on-one with me?"

2. Tell them.

When you know why they're coming to see you, coach them toward a decision. You are the expert.

"After chatting with you, I think the best way to help is to start you with one-on-one sessions. Then you can try the groups if you like the workouts after that. How does that sound?"

3. Emphasize what THEY value.

Talk about the benefits of a one-on-one session to the client rather than the features.

"Our personal training sessions are really affordable" won't have much effect. But consider this alternative:

"Hey Brian, your muscle-ups are getting closer. We work on them about every 2 weeks, but I have an idea: if you have 30 minutes on Tuesday afternoon, I can give you my undivided attention for a half hour. We can do an analysis of your current muscle-up; I'll give you a video and some new things to try. Then I'll give you homework to get you to the next step faster, and you'll be able to do "Nate" as prescribed soon. How does that sound?"

Sounds good to me, and is making major strides toward a first muscle-up worth 40 bucks to your client? Often, the answer is yes.

4. Testify.

The best way to introduce new services is to talk about your experience with the service. Give each of your coaches some 1-on-1 training, and ask them to talk about what they've learned to clients.

Coach to class: "I was struggling with keeping my knees out on the overhead squat, but I did a 1-on-1 session with Jim last week and he gave me a new cue that really helped. So let's all try this: set your stance, and then try to 'spread the floor' with your feet..." Class: "YOU get personal training?!? But you're the coach!" Coach: "Yes, whenever I hit a plateau I need an outside expert to give me coaching. Everyone needs coaching, even us!"

Earlier in this book, I wrote about the salesman's dilemma (the 200lb phone.) The solution, you now know, is to HELP instead of SELL. We can guide a person to the point of decision--yes or no--simply by asking what they want, and then offering to help.

But many will still fear that point of decision. They won't want to lay themselves on the line and ask,

"So, do you wanna?"

because they fear rejection. They're afraid of "no," when (as you've learned,) they should really fear "maybe." Their ego is tied up in their service, and when a potential client says "no" to their service, they take it personally. As you've just read, only the "maybes" can kill you. Help people make decisions, but don't force a "close."

The problem with the "closing" process is that it's like a ping-pong game. You lob up a serve, and the client returns it. Maybe they just drop their paddle and leave. Or maybe they rally for a while, asking questions and probing...but still wind up knocking you flat. The problem: you're on different sides of the net. What if you were on the same team?

I coach people for a living. I coach athletes, kids, CrossFitters, grandmas and business owners. But I NEVER coach the opposing team, because they won't listen. We're in competition. Instead, I coach the kids on MY team, and they do what I ask.

The key to helping someone is to sit on the same bench. Approach a problem on the same team, and make yourself part of the solution.

Scenario: an accountant is about to meet a new client for the second time. On the first visit, he offered a version of the "no-sweat intro": just a chat to offer the client an opportunity to talk about their business. She booked a second appointment, and offered to bring her financial statements.

Dan, the accountant, would like to sign Tiffany, the client, up for his monthly bookkeeping service. He knows its value: when clients file their year-end corporate returns in April, they sometimes arrive in his office with a cardboard box full of crumpled receipts and blurry photocopies. But if they retain his bookkeeping services monthly, he can file their year-ends far more quickly, saving them money. It creates less stress for the client and for Dan, too. Unfortunately, many balk at the monthly fee, though it's barely more than the charges they incur by trying to file at the last minute.

Dan greets the client and asks about her daughter's soccer tournament, which she mentioned at their last meeting. He recalls the tournament because he was paying attention at their last conversation instead of just waiting for his turn to speak. He wasn't waiting to return her serve, but to help her play better. She's impressed Dan remembered.

Dan asks to see her books, and takes a few minutes to carefully review the high and low points. He sees a few areas where he might be able to help: a different tax strategy, a wage subsidy, or maybe upgrading some equipment. So he points those out to offer some value to the client.

"Wow," Tiffany says. "My current accountant didn't tell me any of this stuff."

Dan fights the temptation to smear his competition, knowing it will make him seem less professional.

He's now at the point where, if he were more concerned with "selling" than with helping, he'd go for the "close." There are a thousand ways to do it: the presumptive close, the limited time offer, or the velvet rope. But Dan's not a "closer," and he knows it's not all about him, but her. So he tells her what he would do in her shoes. After all, he's the expert.

"You know, I find it easier to manage my own business when I have another bookkeeper watching over my shoulder every month. He often sees things I don't, because I'm too busy working IN the business to work ON the business," he says.

"YOU have a bookkeeper?!" Tiffany's surprised.

"Of course!" Dan says. "I've found that a monthly check-in with him works best. That way I don't miss any opportunities--and I don't pay any more taxes than I absolutely have to."

Dan's following the same path used by millions of helpers around the world. He demonstrates empathy ("I know how you feel",) experience ("I had the same problem",) and wisdom ("Here's how I solved it.") He's an expert because he's been in the same place and succeeded.

"What would you recommend for me, if you were in my shoes?" Tiffany asks.

"Well, I really like the monthly check-ups," he answers. "For example, if we saw a big tax bill coming in advance, we could do more capital improvement in January. And when April rolls around, your stress level won't skyrocket because we'll be ready for it."

Dan has walked around the desk, physically and metaphorically: he's placed himself on the side of the client. He's demonstrated teamwork. Of course, she might still not sign up, but that's okay; she asked for his opinion, and he gave it honestly. The odds are good that she WILL sign up.

"What does that service cost?" Tiffany asks.

"The monthly plan is two hundred and fifty dollars," Dan says. He doesn't hem and haw, or backpedal, or look away. He knows the value of his service, and he's confident in that value. If she wants more information, she'll ask.

At this point, the salesman will make a fatal error: they'll continue to talk. They'll try to add weight to their proposal with words. But they'll usually sink their own ship, and talk themselves out of Tiffany's business. Not Dan; he's open to questions, but won't waste Tiffany's time by trying to explain the value after he's already demonstrated that value. He won't do her the disservice of turning her into a "maybe." He'll honor her time--and his own--by being black and white about price. No discounts, no special "today-only" deals...because he doesn't have to. He's a professional.

Thanks," Tiffany says. "I'm going to try it out. Is there any kind of contract to sign?"

Of course there isn't: if she doesn't find value in the service, she can leave at any time. This is another hallmark of a professional. A third habit of professionals: they make change easy for their clients.

"I appreciate your faith, Tiffany. There's no contract at all, but if you like, I can take care of the transfer of your books from your current accountant. Can you give me his information, and then sign a disclosure form so he can share your files without any delay?"

Dan offers to shepherd Tiffany right past an awkward conversation with her current accountant, reinforcing his value. This makes her FEEL good, which is more important than anything else.

"People may not remember exactly what you did, or what you said, but they will always

remember how you made them feel" - H Jackson Brown

I try to live the example of "Help First" in my own consulting practice. Over the last several years, I published over 600 free articles for gym owners. I show up and lecture--often for free--anywhere I'm invited. I comment on owners' Facebook groups every few hours, and even build my own wherever I see a gap.

When a business owner wants advice, they can see my calendar online and book a call anytime. I've done over 700 of these calls, and I always pay the long distance charges (even, in one case, to Guam--a $43 call to help someone who won't be out of the Army for two more years.)

I'm not coy with information: I tell the entrepreneur exactly how I'd solve their problem, in their shoes. They benefit from my own experience, but also the experience of hundreds of others. When they ask for mentorship, I tell them my rates, but otherwise there's zero sales pitch.

Over two hundred and thirty business owners have been through my mentorship program (and many continue for years.) NONE have ever asked for a discount. I'm sure many would have been turned off if I'd offered one, because--well, if I'm flexible on my rates, maybe I'm not completely sold on my own advice.

I can afford to be transparent. After all, I don't need the money; my drive comes from a desire to change the world by empowering entrepreneurs. As my wife and I tell our kids all the time, "The purpose of life is to be happy. And you get happy by helping other people be happy."

In another example, Tiffany--invigorated by her meeting with Dan, the accountant--decides to join a gym for the first time. She calls the gym-- let's call it McFitness, because it's a chain--

nearest her office and books an appointment to visit.

Unlike her conversation with Dan, Tiffany is linked to a salesperson right away. Candace is young, fit and seems to know everyone in the club. While giving Tiffany a quick tour of the cardio area, she throws a wink at one of the bodybuilders; touches another on the arm, and stops to talk to a young male Personal Trainer, leaving Tiffany standing awkwardly nearby.

After a four-minute circuit of the gym (including two minutes with the young stud,) Tiffany is offered a chair across the desk from Candace, who glances at her phone before opening up with the sales pitch.

"So Mrs, uh..."--glances at Tiffany's file-- "Chong, what did you think? We have everything, right?"

Tiffany thinks back to the machines: yes, they appeared to have every possible permutation of chrome and steel plate. But if something important were missing, she wouldn't know it: she just wants to gain some energy and tighten up her midsection a little.

"You've gotta try Mike's spin class," Candace gushes. "It's amazing! Total burn. Lots of guys, too!" she grins.

Candace is making a cognitive error: she's putting Tiffany in HER shoes, instead of herself in the client's shoes. She's projecting what she--a young, toned, single girl--wants onto Tiffany, instead of asking what Tiffany wants. Candace is making the conversation about herself, instead of her client.

"So we have three packages," she starts, and rolls off a list of prices from the brochure on her desk. "Any of those really stick out to you?" In other words, the gym sells steak: how much do you want to eat, Mrs. Chong?

"Uh...well, let me think about it..." Tiffany defers.

"OK. Did you have questions I can answer?" Candace asks, returning the ball.

"Not really. I just have to look at my schedule--" Candace cuts her off.

"Well, if you sign up today, I can give you 20% off the registration price. And we can totally spread the payments out over the first year." She leans back, confident in her close.

At this point, Tiffany will leave. But MANY people wouldn't: their low self-esteem bows in the glowing radiance that is Candace. Their ego remembers the cheerleader from high school that wouldn't acknowledge their existence, and they sign on the dotted line because it's what they think they *deserve*. They'll commit to the payments in the belief that money will "motivate" them to show up every month.

It won't.

McFitness calls these people "PIFs"--an acronym for "Paid In Full." Statistically, PIFs who enroll in January are only 43% likely to attend the gym in March. The gym industry is set up to capitalize on PIFs. Every gym makes most of its money on people who never go back.

Every gym, that is, except CrossFit gyms.

I own one of these gyms. We want people to succeed. We don't sell access; we sell coaching. And therapy, for most clients. But many of us make the same cognitive error Candace did: we try to sell the same rare steak to every client.

If Tiffany walked down the street one block, she'd find Catalyst. Inside, she'd meet a bright young coach named Charity, who would ask if Tiffany had time to sit down and chat. She'd probably offer Tiffany a coffee. Then she'd sit next to her, with no desk between them, and pull out a blank sheet of paper.

Our gym's "sales process," is a blank sheet of paper. In the first ten minutes, Charity will ask about Tiffany: why does she want to exercise? Why now? What's she already doing right in life? What does she like? What does she dislike? Who does she like to exercise with?

Then Charity will guide her through Bright Spots, supplying plenty of breadcrumbs--little moments of future joy, as chosen by Tiffany. She'll be asked, "Would you feel more comfortable trying a group, or learning to do CrossFit one-on-one with me?"

Few people ever say "no." Tiffany certainly didn't. I work out with her as part of the "Nooners" on Mondays, Tuesdays and Thursdays. She thanks the coach after every class, and brings muffins for the coaches. Next month, she'll give a "health and wealth" seminar in our gym to help our members with THEIR tax problems.

I'm not a student of metaphysics. But when you spread "Help" to the world, it usually comes back as "Happy."

Confirmation Bias

In general, people seek out evidence to support what they already believe. They don't look for opinion; they look for THEIR opinion to be echoed by you. If you share the same opinion on a solution, they'll believe you. In fact, they'll seek you out.

Why do people go to political rallies? Not because they expect something new from the speaker, but because they want to be in a room full of people who confirm their political opinion. Who shares links about autism and vaccination online? Folks who believe there's a connection. Who reads about scientific studies that "prove" global warming isn't real? People who want to believe it's not real. We confirm our own biases; we don't go looking for "no."

If a client walks into a barbershop and thinks, "A buzz cut would be perfect for this job interview," they aren't looking for an expert opinion. They're looking for confirmation first. The barber might disagree, but the best way to help the client is to start with agreement.

Later in this book, you'll read about "Bright Spots": a method for interviewing new clients and encouraging them to stick with your service for a very long time. The first step in Bright Spots is to confirm what the client is already doing right. A relationship starts when two people take one step in the same direction at the same time. It grows when they take another step, and another. Eventually, they can change direction, but the relationship stays intact if they change direction together.

I'm lucky enough to coach many teens in my gym. Their parents usually attend their first session, which I like. As a parent myself, it's easier to establish authenticity with the adult than with the child.

During the "Bright Spots" conversation, a parent will usually mention how hard they've tried to help their child. They want to impress me with their knowledge. So I look impressed.

"I cook her a good dinner every night: meat, pasta and whole-wheat bread," they'll say. While I'm not a believer in "carb loading," especially for teenagers playing team sports, I'll compliment the parent's efforts.

"That sounds like a ton of work," I say. "I'm glad you pay close attention to what your kid is eating. Most parents don't."

Sometimes the young athlete will interject with a question about a supplement their friends take.

"What about creatine?" they ask, hoping I'll be an advocate for a "miracle" cure. But knowing the parent's approval is more critical than the child's approval in the first meeting, I side with the parent.

"Well, for now, eating what your dad is cooking is best. You need the protein and the energy, because these workouts are going to be hard." I know I'll have months or years to win the athlete over, but if the parent is unimpressed at the first meeting, I'll never have the chance.

"I tell her that same thing," the parent says, without fail. "She just doesn't listen to me. Maybe she'll listen to you."

Then we book the first appointment.

Later in this book is a section called, "The Fire, The Lion and The Darkness." It's really an explanation of propaganda (which is just very effective marketing.) Propaganda works because everyone has cognitive biases. When you uncover the shared belief of a group, it's easy to persuade the group to take action. But I share this powerful strategy because propaganda can also be used for GOOD. It's a powerful tool. Why leave it for the exclusive use of evildoers? Why not use propaganda to help adults quit smoking; help kids get away from screens; help everyone move more and eat better?

Demonstrating "sameness" is establishing authenticity. If you want to coach someone who's adrift, you have to get into the same boat.

What makes you special?

Answer this question: WHY ME?

The average lifetime value of a fitness client can easily top $10,000. If I'm on a gym's website, and can't find a convenient way to ask questions about my knee injury…I'll just ask at the next gym. They'll know the answer.

If my friend Mary recommends you for a massage, but you never answer your phone, I'll call someone else. After all, Mary convinced me that I need massage.

If I can get the same haircut on my block, I won't drive across town for it. Unless, of course, you're special.

Look at your business through the eyes of a new client. What do they see? A great logo? Common language? An easy way to book an appointment? Great.

Now try to find differences between YOUR site and a competitor. Do both use the same language? Do both describe 'fitness' the same way, or show the same models? Same pricing options? Same hours of operation?

Upon first impression, is the only difference between your business and another the price?

New gym clients don't recognize the difference between coaches. They don't understand the word, "community."

New dental clients don't know why your dental work is better than another's dental work.

You might spend a lot of time examining the weakest areas of your business, and that's good. But don't forget what makes you great. Make sure newcomers get that information immediately.

Make a list of your strategic advantages. If there's only one or two, that's okay; make more. In the meantime, trumpet those two.

Examples of strategic advantages:
- First attorney in your area (most experienced)
- Kids program (family-friendly)
- Coaches who have lost weight (we've been in your shoes)

- Stratified pricing model (don't pay for anything you don't want)
- Varied workouts (you'll never get bored)
- Newest office in town (clean, updated equipment)
- Great community (supportive atmosphere, easy to fit in here)

The simple act of writing your strategic advantages will help you focus your branding. You'll differentiate yourself from GloboGym, Mary's Discount Cuts, and other dentists who have a different strategic advantage.

How To Help

"Help First" is a philosophy. When you approach a situation or person with a genuine offer to help, it's still marketing, but it's not the bait-and-switch, Always-Be-Closing philosophy we abhor.

Implementation of the "Help First" philosophy can be split into specific strategies, and then further into precise tactics.

On my blog, I frequently share strategies that WORK--but not down to the finest detail, because that differs from gym to gym.

A strategy is a concept: *here's a person who needs our help*. Tactics are where the rubber meets the road: *here's the way we're going to help them*.

On my blog and in my previous books, you'll read about DOZENS of strategies. Any one could be worth tens of thousands of dollars (some have been worth hundreds of thousands for me.) But I usually save the tactics for our one-on-one mentoring program, the Two-Brain Business mentoring program, and our seminars—until now. Included in this book are ten strategies and several tactics for each!

I'll introduce each strategy first, because I want you to know WHY things work. My goal is to build you a 30-year plan, and it's important for you to understand the WHY so you can change the HOW later. Even when technologies change, the strategies below will still work. In fact, as technology removes more human interaction from our daily lives, these strategies could become MORE powerful.

First, you'll learn about Mavens Strategy, Cobranding Strategy, and Referral Strategy. We'll work through a few examples--tactics--for each. But the real goal isn't to learn how many reps of air squats are done at a Ladies' Night workout; the goal is to learn how to identify a target market, figure out what they want, and use the "Help First" philosophy to deliver it. Strategies are long-term; tactics are short-term. Strategies provide the platform and infrastructure; tactics display your creativity.

"Mavens" are talkers. They're the clients who insist their friends must try your service. They're passionate advocates.

They're NOT salespeople.

When asked, a Maven can convince their spouse, coworkers and friends to show up at your gym, or have their hair cut in your shop. They can sell your wine; they can recommend you. But they won't wear a sandwich board on the sidewalk for you.

If we start the conversation, they'll take it from there. And the best way to start any conversation is an offer to help.

But first, let's give them a reason to love you a *little bit more*. What's the one gift that fits anyone, is always shared and doesn't cost you anything?

It's fame. Putting their name in print. The first step to leveraging our Mavens by starting conversations is letting them talk about their favorite subject: themselves.

Tactic: Maven Stories

Telling a Maven's story on your website is a sure way to start a conversation:

"Hey Mary, I saw your picture on that gym's website last week! You're quite a powerhouse!"

"Hey Bill, I was walking past a mortgage brokerage yesterday and saw your picture in the window! You must have had a good experience…"

"Sam, I was driving down Queen Street and saw that billboard with you on it! Looking good, man!"

Posting a client's story on your website, window (or even a billboard) is a fantastic way to reach their friends and start a conversation. Their face implies a testimonial: obviously, they wouldn't let you talk about them if they weren't completely thrilled with the service.

Importantly, though, we don't use "testimonials" the way we did in the 1990s. Consumers know these are shopped, chopped and sometimes fake. Instead, we tell the story of our clients:

What brought them to our door?
What was their first impression? Has that changed?
How has our service improved THEIR life?
How will our service improve their life in the future?
What's their favorite story about our service?

For example, a Maven who joined our gym might say,

"I thought I had tried everything before I came to Catalyst. But it was different, and I was a bit intimidated at first.
But then I met Chris, and he put me right at ease. Now I'm so glad I took the first step! Being stronger has made me more confident, and last week I finally got the nerve to ask for a raise…and I got it! Now I'll be earning what I'm worth, and coming to the gym more often too! My favorite memory of Catalyst was that time our gym 'adopted' 130 local kids for Christmas. I got choked up, and knew I belonged to a real community, not just a gym."

That example might sound a bit too perfect, but it's typical of the many dozens on our gym website. It's more than a testimonial: it tells a story about an important person, and that sticks with the reader.

Here's another example:

"I finally realized I was in over my head with our bookkeeping, and called Bryan because a friend recommended him.

I was scared Bryan would find all kinds of problems with my do-it-yourself accounting, but he was very patient and actually saved me money AND time.

I was audited last year, and I was terrified. But Bryan was there at every step, and we wound up OK. I actually got a refund of over EIGHT HUNDRED DOLLARS!

I'll be his client for life!"

Later in this book, I'll prove how "sticky" these stories are. But for now, you can take my word on it: everyone loves to see her name in print. And everyone loves to talk about herself. Everyone loves to see social proof. In fact, 80% of the new visitors to my website book their free consultation from the "Client Stories" page, NOT the "Pricing" page or even the "Get Started!" page! Client stories are the most important part of my site.

Start the conversation in these steps:

1. Create an "interview" process. Tell the client you're proud of them, and want to brag up their accomplishments (or simply show them off.) Ask if they'd be amenable to a quick video interview, or if they'd prefer a few written questions.

2. Edit the product (not their responses.) Don't clean up their grammar unless it makes them appear unintelligent. Add a logo to a video, or remove your questions from their answers to create a narrative feel.

3. Publish on your website, and link through social media, email, newsletter, podcast, and in print.

Don't worry about creating perfect media. It's better to get three client stories published every month than to do only one perfectly edited video (or worse, become paralyzed by waiting for "perfection.")

Select three clients every month. Publish their stories. Then consider how you can help others within their sphere of influence.

Tactic: Spheres of Influence

As mentioned above, Oldenburg's research suggests most people "live" the vast majority of their lives in one of three places: the Home (place #1,) the Workplace (#2,) and…the third place.

This "Third Place" is necessary for creative interaction (hobbies or sport,) and typically features a high percentage of regulars, as well as access to food and drink (at least, according to Oldenburg.) It could be a pickup basketball league, a church, or a school.

We'll call each of these three places "Social Bubbles." Each of your clients is at the center of three overlapping bubbles.

With each of the three "mavens" your business is highlighting each month, carefully break down their three "social bubbles":

1. Who do they live with?
2. Who do they work with?
3. Where do they go after work?

Next, consider the other people in those bubbles: What do they want? How can we help them get it?

Tactic: The Car Ride

Q: What's the primary reason I'll sign up for your gym?
A: My wife is already there.

She likes it. The 'trust' barrier has already been overcome. I can spend time with her, find new common ground, AND get all the benefits of exercise.

The simplest way to encourage the spouses and families of your clients to use your service is to invite them.

"Jill, what would it take to get Jack in here for a haircut?"

"Jack, who's doing Jill's taxes for her?"

"Jill, where did Jack buy his last truck?"

Since your client knows their family better than you do, simply asking can often provide hints. What you're really asking is, "Jill, what problem can we solve for Jack?"

Jill might know her husband needs to lose weight. He probably also knows he needs to lose weight; that's not the problem. The problem is that Jack doesn't believe the cost of a gym membership is equal to his need. In other words, he doesn't perceive the cost of exercise to equal the benefit—yet.

We need Jack to try our gym. Jill's on board, but she's tired of "reminding" him about it. Solution: ask JACK for help.

"Hi Jack, we're having an event next weekend, and Jill wants to participate. But she's nervous. We know she'll do fine, but I think it would help if you were around to help. I can give you a job, like scorekeeping, so she's not suspicious. How does that sound?"

Since most people would rather help another person than help themselves, you've given Jack an excuse to be at the gym without feeling any pressure to join.

After the event, we can thank Jack with a coupon for free personal training:

"Jack, thank you. We couldn't have pulled this off without your help. If you ARE thinking about starting, here's a gift certificate worth $200 off our intro package. It expires in two weeks."

You've thanked him. The REAL sales pitch will occur on the ride home, when Jack has to sit in a car with an amped-up maven: his wife, Jill.

If he's ever going to join, it will be within the next two weeks.

Tactic: Help The Kids

If you really want to make me happy, do something for my kids.

For older kids, offer to host their friends or sports team for a free session.

Example: Jill is a maven at my spa who constantly brings her friends in to see me.

"Jill, I just wanted to thank you for bringing all your friends in. I know you have a teenage daughter; what if we invited her friends in for a free group manicure on Saturday in thanks?"

Not only would I win Jill's undying love, but if I sent some information home with each teenager who attended, I'd likely gain the girls as clients…and maybe their mothers, too.

Example: Jill's daughter plays on a local soccer team.

"Jill, I just wanted to thank you for bringing all your friends in. I know your daughter's team is just starting to practice before their season; do you think they'd like to come in for a free mobility clinic after practice?"

Alternately, if their coach is nervous about "sharing" his team with a gym coach:

"Jill, I know a lot of the kids on your daughter's team aren't sure what to eat before a game. I'd be happy to put on a free nutrition seminar for them on Saturday; how can I reach them to send an invitation?"

The key with helping people in your client's "love bubble" is to know who they are, what interests them, and what problems they'd like to solve.

In December 2014, I was delivering a short seminar at a local electricity company. After a short monologue on HIIT and eating well, a staff member raised their hand to ask a question.

"I saw you behind the bench at a hockey game last week," she said. I run the door for the offense on my 7-year-old's team. "Your kids had a ton of energy at 7am! How did you do that?!"

"Well," I replied, "I just wrote up a short nutrition guide for the parents on our team— what to feed their kids, and how to get them to eat it. It's simple stuff."

"How can I get that guide?" she asked.

I smiled. Later, we'll talk about giving away your knowledge through your website, emails and other media.

"Just write down your email address on this napkin," I said. "Anyone else?"

When I posted the guide—called, "How To Feed A Hockey Animal"—on our site, 56 different parents downloaded it in the first week. The next week, two new kids turned up to our Kids' program; their parents had read the guide. These days, we have a waiting list to get into our Kids' groups.

When dealing with the loved ones of your clients, it can help to think, "What can I give them?" instead of "How can I get their money?" This method of peer-to-peer marketing plays on the strongest emotional bond your client has. As you'll read, it's not the most frequent opportunity to get more clients, but it's one of the easiest.

In the last section, I introduced social "bubbles" - groups of people who share something with your clients, or circulate in adjacent circles. Your client has influence over these others.

The first example was the "love bubble": people your client lives with. The next is the "work bubble": people your client works with. Though their influence won't be as strong with a coworker as it is with their husband, there are far more people in this group.

How can we help the coworkers of your client? Our service can provide:
 - A happier workplace
 - A healthier workplace
 - Commonality between staff members ("we all love the same coffee!")
 - A flattening of the corporate structure.

That last one is a biggie. We'll get there.

If your service provides an experience instead of just an appointment, your client will want to share that experience. And teams are built through shared experience: adventures with positive outcomes. This is the definition of "bonding."

Bonding can occur through shared triumph OR tragedy. Luckily, we're in the triumph business, and we can engineer little victories for groups of people, drawing them closer together.

In my gym, we host "Team-building workouts." These feature obstacle courses, little challenges, odd tests (pushing a sled with your friends on it, flipping a giant tire) and short motivational talks throughout. We charge for the service, but the cost is far less than the value. We take pictures of the group during the challenge, and post them on Facebook later. Then we award one "Spirit of Workplace X" prize: five free personal training sessions.

The next day, we email everyone to thank them for working so hard at the gym. "And by the way," we say, "we're looking forward to having Emily in for her free personal training sessions. If anyone wants to join her, there's a printable coupon at the bottom of this email for 50% off our intro program..."

Different services can offer different packages to build the team, of course. Massage therapists can visit an office for 10-minute massages; flower shops can place a bouquet on one random desk every day for a month; hairdressers could host a beard-growing challenge. Restaurants could host a cocktail hour on a secretary's birthday, and invite all of her officemates to celebrate with a free drink.

Dietitians could offer a free 30-day nutrition challenge for an entire office staff, with a downloadable Nutrition Tracking Log (you can download one for free at twobrainbusiness.com, paste your logo into it, and use it yourself!) The point is to offer a special challenge that the team can do together.

One approach might be, "Jill, we want to thank you for being such a fantastic client. And we thought the best way to thank you would be to improve your workplace: make everyone happier, and let you take the credit. I have a couple of ideas for a workplace challenge or seminar; who should I call in your office to set it up?"

Tactic: Thanking The Everyday Heroes

Nurses and teachers are some of my favorite people. Both are under appreciated; one gets you out of serious trouble, and the other keeps you out. In the States, both are underpaid.

Nurses typically work in shifts. Their stress levels are high (and so is their cortisol, making it hard for them to lose weight.) They see the worst of us, and usually bear the brunt of our discomfort. They see death. They can go a full rotation without seeing much sunlight. And they tend to hang out with other nurses.

What if you held a seminar in THEIR workplace at midnight? Or catered in a salad at midnight, when someone usually orders pizza? Or gave a free massage to one nurse on the unit every night for a week?

Next, to invite them to the gym, host a "finale" party after their 30-day challenge. Host a "Nurse's Week" with free gifts (added services) at your business. Or simply send them a "thank-you" card with an offer.

Social Bubbles

While the emotional connection between people in social bubbles is less strong than those in the previous two, the reach of your client is far larger.

Each of your clients has a hobby or passion they can't stop talking about. It could be a bar where everybody knows their name, or golf, or church. And within that hobby are people just like your client: people with jobs and families who probably need your service.

How will your service make each person better at their hobby?
Can your gym improve their golf game?
Can your clothes make them more confident when they're teaching Sunday school?
Can your photography increase their enjoyment of flying model airplanes?

The "Help First" philosophy is easy to apply when you ask the question: "What do they want?" They want more of what they enjoy.

Tactic: Sports Hobbies

There are many ways to improve a golfer's game. Physical training is an obvious way: invite the golfer to bring his foursome to the gym for a free golf-enhancement training session. Offer to help with more golf-specific sessions every week.

But athletes need other things, too: they need the proper equipment and footwear. They need chiropractic care and massage. And they need to look good out there.

Offering a "golf tune-up" at a chiropractic clinic can increase your authority in working with golfers.

Step 1

Ask the client who they've seen in the past. Physiotherapist? Chiropractor? When they give a name, ask permission to share their information with the therapist. Even better, ask them to sign a release of information form on your letterhead. Then tell them you'll call the therapist, "just to make sure I'm on the right track." If you know the therapist well, say so.

Step 2

Create a blank referral protocol. Look professional, and then live up to it. When a RHCP (that's Registered Health Care Professional) shares a client, you won't want to waste their time (or wait too long) with multiple calls for small details. Put it on one form. This is how they do it, too.

Step 3

Ask how you can help the RHCP give the client better service. The biggest highlight of Mike Michalowicz' new book, "The Pumpkin Plan," is that he recommends asking other service providers how you can make their job easier. Find a way to provide service that benefits the RHCP and the client first. Above all, don't create competition; they have to make a living, too. Even overworked service professionals love to give advice; asking, "How can we help get Michael to his appointments more often?" is helping both the RHCP and the client.

Step 4

Make a suggestion, and ask for feedback. A physiotherapist isn't going to write a client's program for you. They're busy, and if you're worthy of their trust, you won't need their oversight. Our initial email, after mentioning the client, looks something like this: "MS mentioned that he's been seeing you for patellofemoral syndrome, and he'd like to get back to playing soccer by the summer. I've recommended two sessions per week for quadriceps mobility and hamstrings strengthening; is that in line with your treatment? Any contraindications we're missing?" Other considerations – Use your letterhead. Don't use a client's full name in correspondence (use their initials, like 'MS' above.) Write professionally, even when you know the therapist personally.

Finally, take them sandwiches.

A professional referral is a big deal. The RHCP isn't just sharing trust; they're risking their own reputation by recommending you. One of my favorite things is having a huge tray delivered, and sitting down with a bunch of therapists for forty minutes to talk about the book or the Ignite program. A professional referral can open a LOT of doors. Therapists interact in a web-like fashion; a typical client case usually carries 4-6 professionals, working as a team. Each professional works on dozens of other cases, with dozens of other professionals.

Entry into this world is tough, but if you've earned a place at the table, it's of great benefit to your business, to other therapists, and to your clients.

One of our primary branding strategies is to establish expertise: to have potential clients view you and your staff as experts in the field of fitness.
I have several strategies toward this end. Some are covered in Two-Brain Business; some are new. One of the strategies really gaining momentum is *cobranding*.
Using your brand to help another brand is great positioning, and a win for everyone.
As you'll see in these examples below, cobranding is helping the business owner by establishing their expertise. It's helping the partner business by pointing their clients in the right direction. And it's helping the consumer make good decisions and learn, learn, learn, baby.

While visiting Virginia, I asked the coach at a local box where I should eat. He pointed me to a local restaurant (let's call it "Lazy's".) He gave me a great recommendation, and I went straight over. When I arrived, I made a discovery: the gym's logo on a decal in the front window of Lazy's. "Box V Approved," it read, and it looked good. The restaurant was fairly upscale, owned locally, and they were happy to cater to the Paleo crowd. On the menus were little green and yellow stickers that said "Paleo" beside a few of the dishes--again, with the affiliate's logo. Very helpful, and a fantastic partnership: anyone trying 'paleo' will learn that paleo-eaters go to box V, and anyone from box V looking for a good meal out will default to Lazy's.

In another food-related cobranding venture, an affiliate in Montana partnered with a local supermarket. Out of driving range of a good farmers' market, they chose Plan B: to help people make the best choices possible in a regular grocery store. They made a two-sided flyer; one side listed ten benefits to eating organically grown food, with the gym logo and website on the bottom. The other side was a map of the store with the organic food highlighted. "Organic strawberries here" read one label; another said, "Organic eggs here." The store sold more organic food; the gym established their expertise in nutrition; the consumer made better choices.

In Tennessee, gym W realized that they could help customers at a local bike store. They write a monthly newsletter email for the bike store's customers. In the email is an 'Exercise of the Month' for cyclists, and a nutrition tip. The store loves it because they can stay in touch with their customers, and provide extra value. The customers love it because they can learn new things for free. Gym W loves it because cyclists show up at their classes.

Back at my gym, we love to host local chiropractors. They talk for thirty minutes on postural issues or stretching, and we record their speech for our members. We 'borrow' their expertise--and their advocacy by association--and their members see our name on the video, too. Other affiliates are going a step further, and placing their monthly newsletters in the chiropractor's office…often with guest posts by the chiropractor. It's a win for everyone.

The key is to approach every cobranding opportunity with, "How can I help?" in mind. Plastering sponsors' logos on your t-shirts or your logo on theirs won't help your cause unless it helps the client.

Cobranding Opportunities

Where do your clients go when they leave your place?

Who cuts their hair? Who sells their clothes? Who does their taxes, cuts their meat or changes their oil?

Your clients need other service professionals. And their clients need you.

Earlier in this book, I used the example of a hairdresser's clients receiving a 20% discount at a nearby dress shop. When two businesses share a market and have non-competing services, it only makes sense to cross-refer.

Your clients trust you. When they confide their nervousness about wearing a bathing suit, they'll welcome your recommendation for a personal trainer. If you're planning their wedding and suggest your favorite photographer, they're very likely to take your recommendation. In fact, you're saving them a lot of stress.

Imagine a bride-to-be in the dress shop. She orders her dress two sizes to small, believing the big deadline of her wedding day will force her to lose a bit of weight. If the shop owner says, "Here's a gift certificate for five personal training sessions at my gym," what will the blushing bride's response be? Probably gratitude.

Likewise, if the same personal trainer invites his female clients to a private showing at the dress shop, who benefits? The shop owner, of course. The clients, definitely. And the trainer will benefit from providing a social experience outside the gym.

The benefits of cobranding partnerships are obvious. The whole is more than the sum of their parts. But there's a difference between true cobranding and advertising.

Cobranding is active: one party overtly recommends the other, and gives their clients a reason to visit. Advertising is passive: a brochure on the front desk, or a business card near the till. Cobranding helps everyone; advertising helps only the advertiser.

Tactic: Weddings

When a young couple gets married, they spend more on professional services than at any other time in their lives. They need a photographer, florist, priest, caterer, decorator, dressmaker, tailor, cake maker and sometimes a wedding planner. Finding each can be tedious--it can also be a big risk. If any link in the chain does a poor job, or doesn't deliver on time, it could ruin everything.

At our gym, we help brides every spring. First, we partner with local wedding planners, photographers and dress shops. We run a "Bridal Bootcamp" to help brides fit into their dresses, and offer two weeks free to women who buy their dress from our partner, or book our photographer. Brides who register with our wedding planner can download our Nutrition Guide and then enjoy the tough-but-fun class for two weeks. The Bootcamp runs 12 weeks, and if they like the first two, they'll usually sign up for the rest. They'll also likely bring their bridesmaids.

The dress shop is happy to have our gift certificates, which are worth $100 each. And the client usually loves the fantastic service we provide. We meet a new client with a strong emotional reason to succeed (the easiest client to train.) It's great for everyone.

How much do you trust your chiropractor?

I'm betting a lot.

If she recommends a nutritionist to help you lose weight, you'll listen. If she hands you a massage therapist's card, you're likely to call. Her recommendation is valuable.

So is yours.

By now, I'm sure you're already asking yourself, "How can I help a chiropractor?" or even better, "How can I help a chiropractor's clients?"

We help chiropractors by giving them a stage. Each month, we host a guest speaker at the gym--we call it the Catalyst Seminar Series-- and rotate through health experts every few months. Chiropractors, physiotherapists, athletic therapists, massage therapists and doctors are invited to teach any topic they like for an hour.

We require preregistration to keep track of attendees (see "Building An Audience" later in this book.) Then we record the speaker, and upload the video to YouTube or another service. The video's title will contain the speaker's name.

When local patrons search for chiropractic care, whose name will pop up first? The chiropractor with the video explaining posture. By publishing the video, we've helped the chiropractor establish their expertise in the market; helped our clients learn more about correct sitting position at their desks; and helped the chiropractor's clients find our gym. The video, of course, will be named "Dr. Smith at Catalyst Fitness," which makes the connection between her service and our own.

There are other ways to help, of course, including cross-referrals for billable client hours. Our IgniteGym program is included in the treatment plans of many local Occupational Therapists, Speech Pathologists and Physiotherapists who work with clients who have brain injuries. IgniteGym bills insurance companies directly, and we refer our clients to these same service providers. If you're providing a professional service in healthcare, building a network of others who serve the same market with a non-competing service is critical.

But we also want to help the other provider's clients. As a gym, our benefit to their clients is obvious: we can keep them moving further from "sickness" and build up a buffer of fitness.

We offer local chiropractors a one-page instructional "How To Squat" brochure. They're busy; they don't have time to show their clients how to do a fundamental human movement. But it's the next step for many of their clients, and when they see a need, our simple brochure can fill it.

The "How To Squat" flyer is one page long with about 200 words and three great pictures. It also boldly invites readers to see a video demonstration on our site (to see it, you can visit www.catalystgym.com/squat.) If they'd like more information, the client can enter their email address to get another useful video on the deadlift.

The client is helped--they can learn how to exercise on their own at home without any commitment. We get to grow our audience, and the chiropractor knows exactly what we're telling her clients.

The Three Stages of Cobranding

As mentioned earlier, active cobranding is far superior to passive advertising. Direct referrals require only three things:

- They must benefit everyone involved;

- They must bridge the gap between the two services;

- They must have a deadline or "call to action."

A good cobranding relationship also has three stages:

- I help you;

- I help your clients;

- You help me.

First, the three requirements of active cobranding:

The partnership must benefit everyone involved: you, the other pro and the client using both.

We had a cobranding agreement with a local oil-and-lube shop. Clients could make a reservation with the shop, and then simply drive to the gym for their workout. A grease monkey would walk over, pick up their car keys and a check, perform the work and have the car back in its parking spot before the client even hit the showers. It was a great benefit to the client and the lube shop, but we didn't push it hard because it didn't work well in the other direction. And the opposite has also been true: some clients who started the Ignite program wanted to stop going to their physiotherapy appointments. Obviously, no physio will want to give a client away forever, so some stopped referring clients.

The referral must bridge the gap between the two services. It's not enough to say, "You should go see Chris! He's the best!" There should be continuity between the two services. Gift certificates can fill this void well. If your hairdresser gives you a gift certificate for five personal training sessions (value: $200) you have a reason to call. And the gift certificate can also create the "call to action" by introducing a deadline: simply add an expiry date.

We offer two gift certificates each to three service professionals each month. To maintain the value of these expensive gifts, we limit both their number and their deadlines.

Our gift offering looks like this: "Hi Mary, we really appreciate the great job you're doing on Sally's stiff back. She raves about you. As a 'thanks' for getting her back in the game faster, here are two gift certificates for $200 each. Give them to your favorite customers as a "thanks," or give them to your staff as a reward--it's up to you. We're so glad you're in town!"

How do we choose the recipients? We start with our own clients.

In our gym, we have a "referral board": a spot for our clients to post their business card. We recommend our clients to our other clients. Who better to build your house than the guy you know from the gym? Who better to sell your house than the guy you met at church? The referral board helps our clients who own businesses or perform a professional service, but also provides a list of cobranding leads every month. We choose three, offer two gift certificates each, and measure their referrals.

The three stages of a cobranding strategy, again:
- I help you;
- I help your clients;
- You help me.

In case you've forgotten, the title of this book is "Help First." That means it's our duty to take the first step toward partnership. We must extend our hand first.

This strategy could also be called "Thank Up." Start the conversation with a "thanks," even if it's just for doing exceptional work. Mention your connection (the client you share) and then the value of your gift. Help them with presentation by telling them what to say when they give your gift to their clients. And help them choose which clients to refer by mentioning their "favorite clients."

Stage 1: Give them a gift certificate to pass along to a client.

Stage 2: Give them a gift to use themselves.

"Mary, thanks for sending John in with that gift certificate. He's exactly the kind of guy we love having in the gym--I can see why he's one of your favorites. But there's one problem: every time he comes to see you, he's going to want to talk about my gym! So now you have to come and try it too. I wouldn't dream of asking you to pay for it, so here's a gift certificate for you, too."

In this example, Mary the chiropractor is more than an afterthought: she's a professional who talks to clients all day. We want her to talk about YOU.

In my world, this is easy because CrossFitters only talk about one thing: CrossFit. If Mary starts doing thrusters on her lunch hour, every person she meets afterward will hear about it. Seth Godin calls these folks "sneezers," because they spread the idea virus to many others.

Stage 3: Give their service to YOUR clients.

"Thanks for the gift certificate," Mary says. "I see some of my clients in your gym. Now how about returning the favor and sending me some of YOUR clients?"

"Of course," you answer. "I'd be happy to. Just give me a few gift certificates to get them through your door..."

You probably see the circle closing here. But wait: there's more.

Mary doesn't just want any of your clients; she wants your BEST clients. And who are your best clients? *Your mavens, of course*. When a maven refers another new client, reward her with a gift certificate to Mary's chiropractic clinic.

Everyone wins when you Help First.

Helping Groups

Over the last few years, I've worked with consulting clients to help them open their businesses with 50, 60, or even 70 members already pre-registered. My all-time record is 94 clients committed in advance (that means the business owner is already holding their check, ready to cash it on Opening Day.)

First, CrossFit Prototype opened with 54 members pre-sold; then CrossFit Belleville took the title with 63. Lowry CrossFit held the record with 70 members enrolled by the end of their Grand Opening day. Currently, CrossFit Apogee holds the title with 94 (but that will likely be broken by a client in Minnesota before you read this book.)

How are they doing it?

By offering extra value to create a sense of immediacy for potential members. By offering pride for early adopters. And it doesn't cost them anything.

Our strategy, in a nutshell:

First, lay the groundwork.

1. Create context. Tell your story on your website and facebook. What brought YOU to try programs? What made you stay? Why did you want to coach? Why do you want to open your own gym? When people feel that they know you a little, it's easier for them to trust you quickly.

2. Establish expertise. Write knowledge-based content. Show the audience your expertise; earn trust before you earn money.

3. Get your website up, and establish your social media presence as soon as you can. Give people a place to go to find answers to their questions.

Next, attract attention.

4. Take your kettlebells to the park, for example. Set up a sandwich board. Run around your parking lot. Wear your box's t-shirt. Take gift certificates to trusted service providers around town. Invite "talkers" to a "free preview" workout. This list is long, and we work through it in the Mentoring Program, but these ideas are all effective.

Offer increased value for a limited time.

5. This sounds sales-y, but it's not. Ask yourself, "How else can I help people get started with my service?" What services will help people learn more about dieting, stick with your program longer, keep their books cleaner, or achieve quicker success?

Offer these for free with pre-registration. For example, members of a gym's Founders' Club might receive one or more of:

- Two free Personal Training sessions (value $180)
- Two free months of Open Gym time (value $100)
- Free admittance to all seminars in the next 12 months (value $280)
- Free admittance to all in-gym events for the next 6 months (value $200)
- Free nutritional profile meeting (value $135)
- "Founders' Club" T-shirt...

It's important to illustrate the price in the above to demonstrate value, because consumers in North America frequently confuse value with price. You and I know the true value of a personalized nutritional plan (about a million bucks!) but for now, you'll have to give your potential clients some context in a language they'll understand (i.e. $135 value!)

Play to their pride.

6. "I was there when this place was a shed in a parking lot..." Founding-member cred is powerful. We have members who still proudly wear their faded yellow 'Catalyst Fitness' t-shirts with a homemade logo from 2005. Green on yellow, thick cotton, and ugly. But they're worn with pride.

Painting your Founders' Club member names on your wall takes guts, but hey – they've committed to YOU. Put their pictures up on your wall. Tell their stories on your site. Celebrate their commitment.

7. My favorite 'Founders' Club' prize so far is a t-shirt that CrossFit Prototype gave its first members. The front has their logo; the back has the member's last name and their member number. For instance, if I'm the eleventh member to officially register, my shirt will say "Cooper" with a big '11' beneath. When a

member wears that shirt, they feel pride…and take ownership of the Box's success, because they're part of the cornerstone.

It seems unbelievable to open a new business with positive cash flow on the first day, but it's happening. The Founders' Club model makes it possible; several boxes are using these very ideas to make it a reality.

The Fire, The Lion and the Darkness: Motivating Groups

When you need to direct a group, you start by controlling their attention. This means providing a focal point ("everyone look at this!") a unifying consequence (a common enemy is easiest) and an emotional reason to believe (usually fear.)

Remember Maslow's Hierarchy? The base of the pyramid was "Security," and that means belonging to a tribe.

elebrate and reinforce membership in the tribe, I'll introduce a strategy called "Social Proof." Basically, you want to show that we're all wearing the same loincloth. In the gym industry, this is means before and after pictures. For a lawyer, this could mean sharing stories of successful business partnerships incorporated in their office. For a chiropractor, it could be a truck driver doing a short video interview about his recovery process.

Social proof shows a potential client a person who seems just like them; it allows the candidate to imagine benefitting from your service. For this strategy, we'll lean heavily on stories.

Testimonials, on the other hand, are those canned pitches you see on most websites. They're usually about a sentence or two long, and usually skimmed by readers. Think about this: the last time you were asked for a testimonial, how did it feel? Or this: what was the last good testimonial you read? You probably don't remember.

We're wired to remember stories. Most of our history as a species has been passed down verbally. That's why you remember the story describing how your grandparents met, but can't recall where you left your keys last night

Focus

Start with common ground: what does the group share? Evildoers often choose biological traits (skin color,) ethnicity or religion. WE can choose a passionate pursuit: fitness, clean teeth, a clean neighborhood or a cause.

By focusing our message on that common ground, we can pull everyone's attention to the same spot. Picture a bonfire in the darkness: your eye can't help but be drawn to it. People like to talk about things that interest them, obviously. When that hobby or cause is significantly different from everything else, it's irresistible to the eye. Contrast helps make this distinction easier. CrossFit is radically different from the rest of the fitness world circa 2000-2010. Eating a higher-fat diet contrasted with medical advice until 2015. Veganism was new once, too.

Counterculture movements are easiest to rally around because they're not the norm. By definition, they attract outliers ("we're not like THEM") as well as first-adopters and revolutionaries. As a small movement ceases to be the exception and becomes the norm, many of these early followers may drop off as the "outsider" draw loses its appeal. Think about functional training in the last decade: the novelty of gymastics rings and snatches in the same workout has become ubiquitous. Every gym has bumper plates now, causing some early adopters to be drawn away toward something else. For them, the newest fire will always burn brightest.

The simpler your idea to understand, the more

attractive it becomes. As you'll read in "Building An Audience," the Early Adopters must have a simple, repeatable message to share with the Early Majority.

Fear

When attention is focused on one commonality, it's easy to keep it. Positive reinforcement ("You're a good person. We're all good people. You're doing the right thing...") keeps attention. From there, it's a simple logical leap to suggest everyone ELSE is looking in the wrong direction.

If you're right, then everyone who disagrees is wrong. Difference is bad; conformity is good. Have you ever noticed that all rebels dress alike?

We're wired to fit into our tribe. We want to belong. So we stoke the bonfire, and commend others who do the same. We start to fear those wandering around out in the dark: "Why do

they prefer the cold? They must be crazy..."
and crazy people do crazy things.

The bonfire is warm and bright. Everything
beyond its light is cold and dark. "Stay close to
the bonfire! Avoid danger and fear!"

Foe

Fear of the unknown is an emotional response,
but can be overcome logically. You might be
scared of the dark, but logic dictates there's no
boogeyman waiting in your basement, so you
slowly descend the stairs. "There's nothing to
worry about," you tell yourself.

But if our fear has a face instead of remaining
an unknown, you'll react differently. You'll take
fewer chances. If there's a lion in the darkness,
you'll stay closer to the fire.

History is full of lions that were invented to
keep villagers close to the fire. Stick to your

puritanical beliefs, or the witches will get you. Don't eat fat, or you'll get fat. Don't touch a barbell, or you'll get big; and don't question your leader, or the cult will board the spaceship without you.

A common enemy unites the tribe, refocusing their purpose and preparing them for battle.

In summary: fire good. Lion very bad. Darkness bad (might contain lion.)

This is a simple concept to apply in your business.

The fire: a unique or novel opportunity, like a charity. Make it as clear and bright as possible. Build the fire so high it becomes hard for anyone to look away. Keep piling wood on top for as long as possible. Capture attention.

The darkness: to your client, any solution is better than no solution. If I provide your workouts every day, then you don't have to guess, or potentially waste your time traveling down the wrong path. Ten years ago, everyone followed the workouts of pros in magazines rather than devise their own; now they follow workouts online. Even coaches follow a small group of other coaches.

The lion: this is the hard part. A common enemy with a face could potentially galvanize your gym community, but a vague threat that's years away won't create an urgency to change.

As an example, consider the efforts of various anti-smoking campaigns over the last 50 years. Which would most likely prompt immediate action:

"Some studies show cigarette smoking might increase the risk of long-term health problems." (No specific consequence, no urgency, passive language)

"Studies show cigarette smoking can cause lung cancer."
(A specific consequence, passive language, no urgency.)

"Smoking makes you stink."
(A specific consequence, passive language, urgent.)

"Smokers stink."
(A specific consequence, active language, urgent.)

We'll discuss the use of active and passive language later. But for now, if you plan to use a consequence in your message, make it an immediate one. As Jerry Seinfeld said,

"According to most studies, people's number one fear is public speaking. Number two is death. Death is number two. Does that sound right? This means to the average person, if you go to a funeral, you're better off in the casket than doing the eulogy."

Obviously, this tactic can be manipulated for evil intent. We don't want to trick people into doing anything; we want to help them and create a win-win situation.

I hate 'selling.' I dislike the connotation. I don't want to be a 'salesman.'

However, I really like sales. I like putting meat, vegetables, nuts and seeds, little starch and no sugar on the table. I like paying my bills. I like positive cash flow. And I like committing my clients to improving their lives.

What is it about 'selling' that conjures up the image of the slick-headed bottom-feeder? Perhaps it's the approach: drip marketing, unsolicited calls, spam, advertising pollution...none of these things make us feel good, right? None of those things helps us pursue excellence, and none of them create value for our clients.

Which leaves us with a quandary: if we build excellent businesses, people will love them. But if they don't KNOW about our businesses, we can't help them.

The answer: help people you don't know.

One of my favorite mentoring clients is Darren from CrossFit Knights. Together, we chose three 'mavens' from among his members and asked ourselves, "How can we help the people they care about?"

One way, we realized, is to provide a nutrition challenge to their coworkers or friends. Here's how it works:

The Approach:

"Hey, Chris. We really like having you around CrossFit Knights, and we want to help your friends get healthier, too. We've got this neat little nutrition challenge that we can run for them; it's simple, they'll feel better, and there's no pressure for them to become members of our gym. What do you think?"

The Plan:

* Host a free seminar on Paleo (or Zone) eating. Keep it simple: focus on eating gluten-free and lactose-free, for example, rather than trying to teach about sleep, supplementation, nightshades, and the rest.

* Derive a simple points system: 5 points for a day of perfect pale; 3 points if the participant missed a meal; 1 point just for being nice (never give a zero.)
* Put up a whiteboard with your logo in their workplace. Let them log daily scores, and ask questions of your gym member with whom they work.
* Give the 'winner' a free month or starter package.

The Benefits:

* Non-members are participating as members of your gym. This helps make the mental transition from 'outsider' to 'insider.' Cults use this same tactic, and it's powerful. We're using this superpower for good, however.
* New people can interact with your brand every day without being faced with a purchase decision.
* Your existing client can become an ADVOCATE without becoming a SALESPERSON.

* After a month, you've pre-qualified the non-member most likely to become engaged in your program.
* It's easy to make a transitional offer to participants. "Want to feel even better? We'd be happy to host you folks for a free workout on Saturday." You're demonstrating that you can make complex things simple to understand.
* You're helping people.

Question: what's a 'good' drip? The one you don't get.

You don't want a drip from your roof. You don't want a drip from your organs. You don't want drip marketing from salespeople, and neither do your clients want a daily "sign up now…you know you want to!" from you.

What's Helping?

OnBoarding: Turning Strangers Into Long-Term Clients

It might seem as if clients appear randomly at your doorstep. But there's really a broad pattern to all your relationships.

The pattern takes place in four distinct stages—Attention, Desire, Integration and Retention—and though clients pass through at different rates, knowing where to spend your time means far greater return on your "help" investment.

In a later section, I'll provide a tool to measure your OnBoarding process. You'll see where your marketing is strongest, and identify opportunities for improvement. This has streamlined my own efforts and greatly "unclogged the funnel" of new clients.

Stage 1: Attention

Clients are walking past your brand all the time.

Maybe this is happening literally, but maybe you have dozens--hundreds--of local people paying attention to what you're doing. They're standing on your stoop. They just haven't found the right reason to ring your bell--yet.

Wouldn't you like to know who they are? Or why they aren't knocking?

A peephole into the world your clients inhabit is priceless. You want to know who you're helping: where do they work? Are they married? What do they like? How much do they value their health?

You have answers. They have questions. Help them...and ask their name while doing so.

If you can organize them into groups, that's even better.

First, we need to give them something that helps. This is where publishing free content comes in: it's useful, it solves their problem, and it's easy to understand. You're helping them, and they'll appreciate it. So shake their hand: let them introduce themselves before walking away.

When a potential client sees information they like--for example, a guide to weight loss--they'll download it. Before they do, get their information: put your best content behind a registration form. If you're already using booking software for your business, this is easy to do: just have the client register online, "buy" the information package for free, and send them a link to download in their emailed receipt.

In late 2014, we started to notice increasing interest from the less-hardcore fitness crowd. To prepare for the 2015 Resolution Season, we created a "2015 Fitness Guide" for our City. We allowed the organizers of different events to list their dates inside, and we gave training recommendations for each. Then we planned specialty training groups for each. For example, if a local Midnight 5k event was scheduled for July 1, we'd start a 5k training group around May 15, and put both in the Fitness Guide. We'd publish tips for runners, Obstacle Course racers, fitness competitors, and football players...and links to sign up for help.

We published the Guide on a hidden page on the CatalystGym.com site, and then promoted it with a post. The post promised free access, and had a link to sign up to receive the downloadable PDF. When people registered for the Guide, they were auto-emailed a link to the hidden page. Then they downloaded our Guide (full of tips and links to register for Catalyst services) and kept it around all year.

Second, their information was automatically added to our Newsletter list. Every month, they received some stories from Catalyst (social proof,) an exercise tip (establishing authority) and links to register for our beginner's program, personal training or CrossFit.

Third, as we began to accumulate data, we could see who our primary followers were. This allowed us to tailor our offerings depending on the time of year; add new courses; or eliminate courses for which the market didn't match the service were wanted to provide. For example, if interest waned in our Obstacle Course Racing program, we stopped offering it and replaced it with Campfire Guitar, or another service that better matched our target market.

Fourth, we created groups on social media as "collectors" for our information. Rather than name the group after our business, we named the groups according to the goals of the client: "Weight Loss in Philly," "Get Fit 2015 In Texas," or anything else clients might want. We posted links to our content in these groups, answered questions, and generally tried to help. This let us draw a circle around those who were paying attention to our brand, and raise awareness among those who weren't.

You don't need such a comprehensive document to get started. Instead, you can use simple blog posts or videos--still valuable content--and the booking system you already have to gather this information. From there, you can start delivering your message to previously unknown audiences.

The difference between a borrower and a thief is that a borrower leaves his name behind. Let's make sure we're lending information instead of leaving it in a basket on the stoop.

Stage 2: Desire

What makes your service desirable? Demonstration of expertise, a sticky story, and value.
If you visit the CrossFit facebook page, you might notice their "listing type:" a Media company, not a fitness company. CrossFit HQ

has a staff of hundreds of content producers: writers, editors, videographers, producers, cameramen and social media experts. They're incredible at what they do (and, for the most part, excellent people.)

The content produced at their office in Santa Cruz, CA is high-quality, and falls primarily into two categories:

1. Stories of people doing CrossFit;
2. Expertise to establish CrossFit's authority as THE expert in fitness.

Starting with Greg Glassman, who entered the crowded fitness marketplace in 2001, CrossFit Media has produced high-value content every day for 15 years. That's remarkable. There's no better single source for knowledge in the fitness industry. I even created a tiny fraction of it!

The reason many coaches trust CrossFit is its rigid approach to publication: no shady science, no salesmanship, no fear.

Occasionally, feelings are bruised in political correctness is lost in unapologetic social media posts, but real leaders occasionally make their followers uncomfortable. Sometimes a left- or right-wing statement helps pull people back to center. And sometimes challenge for the sake of challenge is a good thing.

The stories of athletes—including grandmas, football players and kids—doing CrossFit workouts are the sticky part. Readers LOVE to see videos of 80-year-olds lifting weights, or 30-year-olds lifting huge weights. Fitness coaches love to see old perceptions shattered. Cynics (like me) love to see "gurus" exposed. As another famous coach, Mel Siff, once said to me in a private email:

"If you plant your flag, people will start shooting at it."

CrossFit HQ offers a unique and desirable proposition: for $3000 per year (currently,) a wannabe entrepreneur can license one of the most powerful brands in the world. CrossFit, Inc.'s responsibility is in the first stage of the OnBoarding process (Awareness,) and they've done a great job. But the SECOND stage is the responsibility of the licensee.

In short, a gym owner's job is to become renowned as the local health and fitness expert who chooses CrossFit. Their role is to explain to Tom, Tiffany and Theresa how CrossFit can solve the weight loss problems of Anytown, USA.

This is the stage where content marketing is critical. Demonstrating how your service can solve the problem of a potential client is what's required to gain that client. Knowing your client's problem is paramount. Use the "Target Markets" section to determine future clients, and then put yourself in their shoes: what information will help them find you?

Stage 3: Integration

In the Integration stage, the client makes the decision to fit your service into their calendar, their budget, and their thoughts. They're no longer just paying attention: now they're paying money.

Prior to this stage, the client has passed through the Awareness stage (they've heard of you,) and the Desire stage (they've seen what you've done in the past, and wonder if you can do the same for them.) Both stages have been discussed at length already.

My integration and retention system is called "Bright Spots." I stole the idea from researchers at Carnegie Mellon and Harvard Universities (George Lowenstein, and Chip and Dan Heath, respectively.) "Bright Spots" is a behavioral modification strategy, NOT a sales strategy.

The first "Bright Spots" opportunity occurs at the transition point between the "Desire" stage and the "Integration" stage. This is where we first meet the client and ask the most important question of all: "How can I help?"

In the section, "What do THEY Want?" I wrote about the importance of knowing the answer to this question before recommending any service. What's the benefit sought by the client? That's our starting point. Sell the benefit of your service, NOT the features: don't simply list a menu of what you're selling.

For example, If a client wants to look professional for a job interview, he needs you to say, "You need a more conservative haircut and a shave." The alternative—telling a client, "I sell haircuts, trims, waxes, styles, perms, shaving and coloring"—leaves him alone to make the connection between what he wants and what you can sell him. He probably doesn't KNOW what he needs; you do.

To begin, the client has to trust your judgment. He must first decide you have his best interests in mind. He already knows what you KNOW; now he needs to know that you CARE. So I start the process with a question:

"How can I help?"

When most service people ask this same question, they're really asking, "What do you want to buy?" But not me: I want to know how the client will view success. So I take notes as they're speaking to demonstrate how important their goals are to my recommendation.

Consider the difference between these two questions:

"What service do you want me to perform?"

"What outcome will my service create for you?"

The second question is where the client begins to make an emotional connection to your service. If the gentleman preparing for a job interview can see himself getting the job after using your service, you'll create a stronger bond. So the first question necessary for behavior modification is:

"What will success look like?" In other words, "If I do a great job on your hair, what will happen?" He'll impress his interviewer and get the job.

The second question in the behavioral modification process:

"Where are we starting from?"

It's important for the client to know he's already doing something right; that he's not starting from ground zero. This creates momentum that will lead to fulfillment. In this case, the hairdresser might say, "You already have very clean and soft hair; what are you using for shampoo and conditioner?"

Her praise will be the client's first "Bright Spot," and start the foundation of trust. The praise must be genuine, and reinforce what the client is already doing WELL.

Next, the hairdresser makes a recommendation based on the client's goal (benefit of service) and Bright Spots (what they're currently doing.) She also sets the stage for retention by asking, "If this goes well, what kind of job are you hoping to get?" I'll write more on this step later in this book.

She can also help the client maintain their new look with a few tips before they leave. But the next step—the follow up—will set the hairdresser apart.

After the client leaves the shop, the hairdresser can type a quick email—"Well? How did it go? Did you get the job?"—and schedule it to send for a date after the client's job interview. This requires less than 30 seconds of work, but will reinforce the level of trust and care between the two. When the client responds, they'll give either a positive ("I got it!!") or negative ("I didn't get it.") which creates an opportunity either way.

In the first instance ("I got it!!") the hairdresser can simply congratulate the client and include a booking link for his next appointment. In the second, the pro can offer her condolences and add, "Tell me all about it as soon as you can. Here's a link to my schedule – see you soon!" The client still knows their hairdresser cares, and has a clear path to booking the next service.

In the gym, clients start with a conversation: what have you done before? What do you like? What do you hope to achieve? From there, goals can be split into small micro-goals (Bright Spots,) and attached to emotions ("How will losing five pounds make you feel? How will others react? What's the first thing you'll notice?") Follow-up calls and emails reinforce client successes.

For a more in-depth discussion on Bright Spots in the fitness industry, see "Two-Brain Business 2.0."

When clients are successful, they want others to know. What good is a gold medal without a podium to stand triumphantly atop?

Stage 4: Retention

In Sweden, blood donors get a text whenever their blood is used to help someone else. They also get an automatic "Thanks!" text when they donate, but the confirmation text is far more important. It tells them giving from their veins was not in vain, encourages repeat behavior and makes them feel important.

There are two important metrics to track in a long-term client relationship:
1) Adherence – how often the client uses the service;
2) Retention – how long the relationship lasts between first visit and last.

Both are equally important. A client who visits the library five times in their first week and then disappears isn't an ideal client. Likewise, a client who makes an annual visit for five years isn't really receiving the best service they could be.

Service pros work at all parts of the "adherence" spectrum. Nutritionists must have high adherence, because their clients won't succeed if they don't stick to their diet every day. Hairdressers have lower adherence: their clients attend every two weeks. And wedding planners have very low adherence: 50% of their clients will only use their service once! Some professionals must also encourage adherence when the client is outside their care. Dentists book quarterly appointments, but their clients must adhere to a regular routine of brushing and flossing. Personal trainers might give "homework" for their trainees to follow between visits.

The number of clients required to sustain a business is inversely proportional to its adherence rate. If you have a low adherence rate, you need more clients. If you have a high adherence rate, you simply can't take more. Naturally, a business that sees its clients every day will charge more. No professional can effectively help 300 people every day; if they can help five in a day, they need to make a living from those five.

Adherence is also a double-edged sword: when a business undercharges for its service, and adherence is high, the owner's time becomes less valuable. For example, if I pay a gym $100 per month to attend classes, but attend six classes per week, my rate per class is only a little higher than $5. If another client, paying the same $100 per month, attends only twice per week; their value per visit is much higher (just over $12) but they're less likely to achieve the results they seek.

Fill a gym with clients who will attend six times every week, and you'll need more coaches, equipment and space. People will become more fit, but the business will become unsustainable (more on this in Two-Brain Business and Two-Brain Business 2.0.) But fill a gym with folks who attend twice per week, and long-term retention will be low because they won't see results.

Adherence requires balance and constant measurement.

When clients see their financial planner once every year, they don't form a meaningful relationship. It's easy for the client to be swayed to another planner, or worse—to become convinced they can "do it themselves" and start trading stocks online. A higher adherence rate (quarterly meetings) will help with long-term customer retention, because the client will perceive a partnership with their planner.

When the stock market tanked in 2008, I didn't hear anything from my financial "advisor." I received annual updates—with mounting rage, I should add—but didn't get a call, or even an email. I felt abandoned, so I went elsewhere.

Adherence doesn't always require face-to-face meetings. In the Internet age, regular communication is easy (and sometimes it's even automated.)

Research indicates a "hierarchy" of conversation for strengthening relationships:

1. In-person
2. Over the phone
3. Text message
4. Email
5. Notes.

In-person conversation is strongest because it seems more genuine. We do most of our communicating without words, and a face-to-face congratulation will feel most sincere. A phone call is still good, as it's a two-way line; so, debatably, is text messaging. But email can become a one-way conversation, and notes don't elicit a response.

Planning for regular updates with clients is best for adherence. An appointment to meet face-to-face is best, but a phone conversation is encouraging. Text messages and Facebook messaging are best done one-on-one instead of in a group.

If all else fails, set up emails that will automatically send at regular intervals. This is a last-case, can't-do-anything-else, bottom-of-the-barrel tactic, but it's better than nothing. A regular email might keep the conversation alive (though barely) until another in-person appointment can be made.

Knowing what a client really wants is important at all stages of Onboarding. Reminding the client they got what they wanted—and you helped—is critical for long-term retention. In the previous example, the hairdresser asked the client, "If I give you a good haircut and shave, what kind of job are you hoping to get?" This forms a psychological link between the successful outcome and the provider's help: the client will recall how important the haircut was to the first impression of his new bosses. When the hairdresser congratulates the client's success on social media, the client's friends see it. Other clients see it. Everyone sees this message: HAIRCUT = SUCCESS.

The hairdresser can use the "Podium Week" tactic to highlight the newly-employed client. In the fitness industry, retention is notoriously low. A client who joins the gym on January 1 is only 43% likely to attend after the first three months. The gym industry doesn't work to improve this statistic; instead, most chains take advantage of the client who isn't self-motivated. They offer low monthly rates in exchange for a front-end "registration fee." New members, feeling motivated, commit themselves and begin to attend. But as their motivation wanes, they stop attending…but can't cancel out of their contract. And this is the way most commercial chains WANT it, because if every member showed up every day, their equipment costs would triple. CrossFit works better for many reasons, but retention is a big one. A CrossFit gym fails when its clients stop attending. The price is much higher, but the gym's success is tied to the client's success instead of up-front sales and marketing. It's critical for owners of small-box gyms to know the goal of each client

BEFORE prescribing a solution, and to reinforce the "wins" regularly.

Tactic: Moving To Objectively-Measurable Goals

Every client is a psych patient.
At their first visit, a new client is a mess of emotions. Their ego is on the defensive, because they're admitting to know less than you do. They're also worried you'll make fun of their inability to balance a checkbook or lose weight.
First, highlight what they're doing right.

Tactic: The 20% Bonus

Showing a new client they're already on the road to success can build much-needed momentum. In the gym, highlighting a touchstone exercise at which the new client excels can keep them coming in more regularly. Teach a woman to do double-unders? She'll show up for every workout where you incorporate skipping techniques, because she's already good at it. Got a tall guy in OnRamp? Let him deadlift a decent weight before he starts CrossFit. Whenever a deadlift comes up, he'll show, because that's "his thing."

Two studies quoted in "Switch," by Chip and Dan Heath, illustrate the benefit of giving people a 'head start' - or making them aware that they're "gifted" before they get rolling. In one, researchers quizzed hotel room cleaners about their daily exercise levels. Despite their high work output daily - they're moving quickly through hotel rooms, with a time limit, for 8 hours per day, with gear - most described themselves as a "non-exerciser" because they weren't members of a gym. Their work output, though, was quadruple the typical half-hour on a treadmill. CrossFit? No, but much tougher than the workout of most gym-goers. Here's the beautiful part: when researchers made the results known to the cleaners, they dropped an average of 1.8lbs in the next month, without changing anything else. They didn't join gyms; they didn't eat better; but they worked harder, because they were exercising. 1.8lbs doesn't sound like much, but in a huge sample, it's significant, especially when food and other variables are controlled.

In the second study, patrons of a car wash were given a new punch card to earn free cleanings. One group was given an 8-punch card; after they'd accumulated 8 punches, they got a free wash. The other group was given a 10-punch card, with two punches already tallied. They, too, had to earn 8 more punches before they could get a free wash.

After three months, the second group was twice as likely - 36% to 18% - to have filled their cards. There were no other differences between the groups, other than the 20% bonus.

If you're trying to keep someone at your business longer, why not exploit their strengths? Even better, brag 'em up in public! Clients aren't only new to your business: they're new to setting goals. They don't KNOW how much easier bookkeeping can be if they keep their receipts in order. They don't know WHY their bras don't fit well, or why they can't lose weight. They don't know ANYTHING about the guitar.

Their goals are uneducated, and therefore subjective: they say, "I need to lose twenty pounds!" because they recently saw that number on a magazine cover. Or they'll say, "I need a refund of $2000 on my taxes," because that's what they qualified to receive last year. Just like a new recruit in the army, they've never learned how to sight in their rifles.

New clients need help setting goals. Our job is to coach them toward their first "bright spot." First, find something at which they excel.

Personal trainer: "Wow, you're a natural at deadlifting – that's 95lbs on your first day!"

Bookkeeper: "Your files are well-organized, so we can make progress really quickly here."

Insurance sales: "You're more savvy than the average client, so we can customize a plan around what you want instead of using the choices we normally give."

Chef: "You have great taste in wine. How are you at matching your wines with your meals?" After we've identified a strength, we can ask about their NEXT achievement. We call these "Future Bright Spots," and if you read the previous section on Podiums, you'll know what's coming next.

Personal Trainer: "...that's 95lbs on your first day? What are you going to do next?" Client: "A hundred pounds!" (goal)

Bookkeeper: "...we can make progress really quickly here. What would you like to accomplish within the next week or so?" (goal)

Insurance sales: "...customize a plan around what you want instead of using the choices we normally give. What do you want your new plan to cover?" (goal)

Chef: "...matching your wines with your meals? What's your favorite cut of beef for that particular red?" (goal)

At each stage, the client becomes better at sighting in their rifle. They're identifying small, achievable goals that will act as bread crumbs on the trail ahead. The best part: every time

they achieve one of these "bright spots," they'll
THANK YOU for it.

Client: "I did it! One hundred pounds! Thanks,
Coach! You're the best!"

Client: "Wow, I actually got my income taxes
finished in five days! Thanks for the deadline!"

Client: "I feel better knowing my family is
covered if something happens to me. Thanks,
Bob."

Client: "That steak was PERFECT for my
favorite wine. Thanks, Chef!"

In case you missed the subtle psychological
shift happening, the client moved from a
subjective (almost random) goal to a clearly-
defined, objectively-measurable goal. This is
important for adherence: when people are
successful, they keep going. When they're not
successful, they stop.

The Globogym industry has no such Bright
Spots. You can't "win" at the pec deck. There
are no podiums, no tiny microgoals, no follow
up from an expert. Even if you're not in the
fitness industry, any large-scale competitor to
your service can't possibly deliver the retention

strategy you now know.

This is your competitive advantage: transformation of a client's goals first, then transformation of a client's habits, then transformation of a client's life.

After their success, have them forecast their own "bright spot": a micro goal of their own invention. Since they "own" the goal, they'll form an emotional connection to success under your guidance, and the REAL long-term retention strategy begins…

Tactic: Moving To Emotional Attachment

Your clients might be your friends, but they also pay you money.

Many service professionals imagine a deep interpersonal relationship with their clients. This isn't wrong: the service professional cares deeply, and presumes the client feels the same way. But the dollar barrier prevents true emotional attachment. After all, your best friends don't pay you to be their friend.

Rather than hope every client likes you enough to stay forever, we can forge an emotional attachment between the client and their goals. Emotion is much stronger than logic. We all know we shouldn't smoke; should lose a few pounds; should exercise more. But we don't DO any of those things until we have an emotional reason.

Here's the best example I have: a new potential client came into my gym with his wife. She was already exercising regularly elsewhere, and nagged him to find a gym. He thought Catalyst might be the best way out of a bad conversation. He obviously didn't want to be there, but showed up to a few group classes and then petered out.

A year later, he came rushing into my 6am class as it was about to start. He put his head down and hammered through the workout until I told him to stop. He lay on the floor for almost twenty minutes trying not to throw up. When he finally stood to hit the showers, I asked him where the new motivation was coming from.

He hemmed and hawed, but finally admitted: "I think my wife is cheating on me."

THAT'S an emotional reason to exercise.

Every accountant has a similar story: the last-minute tax client who won't turn in their monthly paperwork, won't keep receipts and can't keep a schedule—until they get audited. Then, scared, they're desperate for help; cost no longer matters. Like a repentant drinker, they vow never to sin again. And if they find other emotional reasons to stay straight, they never will.

Part of my work in the IgniteGym program involves veterans with PTSD. On average, 22 vets kill themselves every day in the U.S.—a terrifying number. But many more veterans THINK about killing themselves and DON'T do it. What's the difference? Usually an emotional connection stronger than their depression: they don't want to orphan their kids, or widow their wife. When logic won't cut it, emotion might. Every client is a psych patient.

After they've found success under your care, ask them a very important question:

"What are you going to do NEXT?"

Frame the question with a reminder of previous success (I called this "The 20% Bonus" in a previous section.)

"Wow, you did it! You deadlifted a hundred pounds, and made it look easy! What are you going to do next?"

"Great job getting those taxes done! You do well under pressure. What would you like to tackle next?"

"I think this insurance plan is perfect – you've covered all the bases. What's the next step toward retirement?"

"Your steak choice was perfect for that wine. Can you do as well with your dessert choice?"

These are tiny goals; baby steps. And just like babies, clients require a lot of praise in the early stages. Praise can come from any feedback (follow the hierarchy above,) but should be immediate.

In our gym, we keep a "PR board" for client Personal Records. When any client reaches a new achievement, we write it on the board: "Wow, Mary, have you ever done that many box jumps in a minute before? No? Let's write it up here!"

This provides social proof, a podium for the client AND a good reason to call them later.

"Hey Mary, it's Bill from Catalyst. I just saw your box jump PR from last Tuesday! We're so proud of you! What are you going to do next?" (goal)

It's a simple process in fitness, but it can be done in any service business.

"Hey Mary, I saw from your Facebook posts that you got the job! Way to go—and your hair still looks fantastic! What's the next big occasion?"

"Hey Mary, I was just notified by the IRS that you got that tax refund! You're making progress! What's the next big opportunity you'd like to tackle?"

Hey Mary, after that big rain last night I thought I'd call to congratulate you on that new roof. What's the next home-repair project?" These are the most powerful sales calls you can make. But NONE of them feel like sales calls! After all, you're just helping, and then praising.

Tactic: Help Again

Eventually, every client drops off.
This can happen after a few visits, or after years. The difference can be astronomical: a ten-year client is worth thousands of dollars, and is easier to service. Conversations are no longer confined to small talk. You'll be invited to their kids' weddings, and the connection will benefit them, too: you'll likely been a much-needed confidante (or therapist) when they need objective advice.
But your friendly banter might not be enough. Novelty is a powerful motivator, and when a client feels bored, they're gone. When they want something "fresh," they might seek out a new dress shop or dentist. When their workout

is no longer exciting, they'll seek a new gym. And when their car starts to die, they'll look for something different at another dealership.

Your "old clients" are the easiest "new clients" to get IF you reaffirm their emotional connections to their goals.

Here's how we handle it:

When a gym client goes missing for two weeks, we add them to the "absentee" list. On Friday afternoon, we call them and ask if they're progressing toward their goals (Future Bright Spots, as spelled out above.)

We don't say, "Where are you?! We miss you so much!" because that would mean playing on an emotional connection that obviously doesn't work both ways. Instead, we go straight to the emotional connection they DO have: to their Bright Spots.

For example:

"Hey Mary! Bill from Catalyst here. Just checking to see if you're getting any closer to that goal of deadlifting a hundred pounds…"

Mary's response will give us insight into how we can help again.

Client: "No, I've been coming to class but not getting any closer."

Bill: "No problem, Mary. Are you free to chat next Tuesday? We can set up a new plan for the summer and just let that deadlift goal sit for awhile, just to keep things spicy."

Example 2:

Mary: "Yes, I reached that goal last week."

Bill: "Fantastic! What are you going to do next?"

Example 3:

Mary: "No, I haven't. To be honest, I'm not sure this is for me."

Bill: "No problem. It's not for everyone. Would you like to talk about Personal Training instead?"

Whatever Mary's response, she's created options for further conversation. She's still paying attention; still in the story.

We have several clients who have reached the ten-year mark, and one who hit Year 13 in 2015. Ask them why they stay, and they'll respond, "It's different every time I come in."

Their perception of novelty isn't perfectly accurate (everyone repeats workouts sometimes) but because their goals stay ahead of their workouts, they're never bored.

This can work for any service provider. Example:

"Hey Mary, I know you're trying to grow your hair longer over the winter. How's that going so far?"

"Hey Mary, I know your plan was to buy a second rental property after you found tenants for the first. Is the first building full yet?"

"Hey Mary, I know your goal after that income tax refund was to cut your tax burden by incorporating your business. Have you done that yet?"

In each case, we can offer help with anything they say. That help can be their next "Bright Spot," and the relationship can regain its former momentum.

Long-term clients are the backbone of any service business. It's easier to keep a client than to gain a new client. But if we fail to work hard at retention, and spend all our time marketing instead—well, we'll spend all our time marketing instead.

The Growing Tail

Chris Anderson's book, "The Long Tail," is about making goods that stand the test of time and capitalizing on the long-term audience. To Anderson, the initial spike in product interest is good, but a slow taper in interest is where the real opportunity lies.

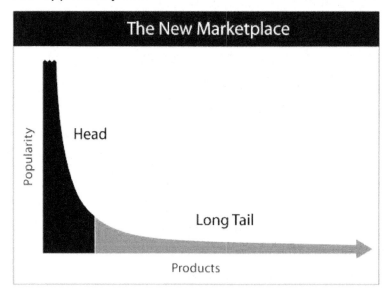

When the original "Star Wars" movie launched on May 25, 1977, it grossed $1,554,475 in its opening weekend—not bad for a new concept forty years ago. That's the "Head" you see on the graph above. But the "Long Tail," representing sales since opening weekend, totals $786,598,007. And combined with the next five "Star Wars" films, the total gross revenues are $4,494,909,673. That's "Billion" with a capital "B." Though sales of the "Star Wars" film are less per DAY than they were on opening weekend, the series continues to sell well over time. This is the effect of the long tail on PRODUCTS.

We're selling SERVICES. The long tail concept still holds, but looks very different. In fact, our tail goes UP, not down. Our clients, ideally, will spend money at an increasing rate over time: they'll benefit from our help and increase their use.

"Wealth" can be described as "value for time." Wealth can be created though the sale of goods by increasing the number of goods sold through ramped-up production. But your "good" is your time, and you can't increase production of your time. The only path to wealth in the service industry is through increased value. For most of us, that will mean focusing on fewer clients who carry higher value.

As an example, consider the choice made by a hairdresser: three clients who want a simple cut for $20 (requiring about 15 minutes each;) or one client who wants a full 'do for $99 but requires 45 minutes of service time. Obviously, the second option is better. Counting the time required to process each payment, get the next customer into her chair and make small talk, the second service is far more valuable. It might be harder to find the $99 client, but not impossible; over time, the hairdresser should move toward helping fewer total clients with a higher percentage of $99 clients.

The total number of clients will decrease, of course, but the average revenue PER client will dramatically increase. This moves the hairdresser closer to wealth, stops the cycle of market/cut/market, and shortens her workday.

Discounts have the opposite effect, as discussed later in this chapter. For more on this topic, see the Two-Brain Business series.

Creating Audiences

What's the difference between a busker and a musician?

The musician has an audience.

The busker finds a location and starts playing. She doesn't know who will pass by that day, but depends on the interest and generosity of strangers. She has no set value or minimum bid; people are left to determine her worth based on their own experience and preconceptions.

A musician's audience is pre-committed. They purchase the tickets--priced by the musician based on HER experience--and own the seat. If they don't show, she still gets paid. If it rains, she still gets paid. And her live performance is just a pathway to her real asset: the album she's selling.

Though the revenue from the show is nice, we're mostly concerned with selling the asset. As Chris Anderson writes in "The Long Tail," lifetime value of the client dwarfs the first sale. Sometimes it's worth giving the first performance away free to create an audience. The key is to get everyone in one room and paying attention, even if they're not yet paying you money.

Imagine this: a dozen people waiting for you to announce your next service so they can sign up. Pre-registration lines. Folks hitting "refresh" on your website so they can be first to buy. We've become accustomed to seeing this type of anticipation for products like video games and iPhones, not for services--but it is possible. Creating an audience means:

- Education (who you are, and what you're doing)
- Inspiration (you have the answer to their problem)
- Anticipation (excitement, or buzz.)

If we review our OnBoarding process (Awareness / Desire / Integration / Retention) we'll see a strong overlap with the process to create an audience. That's no accident: the OnBoarding process is the foundation on which we plan and measure our marketing. Specific strategies are laid on top of the Onboarding plan, and then tactics on top of the strategies. The "Awareness" phase is where most advertising focuses. Ad salesmen will frequently cite "getting your name out there" as the most important part of marketing. But with a heavily overpopulated marketplace, your brand has to be more than seen: it has to be liked. Your first impression must create affinity. What makes people like you? Helping them. The best first impressions are created with the "Help First" philosophy.

If one of our target markets is "Fat Loss," we can build our audience through:

1 Free seminars on fat loss;

2 Free information published on our site;

3 Free nutrition tracking logs (giveaways)

4 Partnerships with other professionals who serve the same market

5 Public "Fat Loss in NYC" Facebook groups

6 "Fat Loss Tips in NYC" Instagram and Twitter accounts

7 Columns in local newspapers and media

8 Interviews on local podcasts and radio

9 Guided grocery shopping tours in local

supermarkets

10 Appearance at farmers' markets

11 Supplementary menus in local restaurants

12 Fat loss challenges at our gym or with local partners

13 Partnerships with local farmers

14 Specific newsletters to a "fat loss" subscribers' group

If one of our target markets for our accounting business is other entrepreneurs, we can build our audience through:

1 Free seminars on tax savings

2 Downloadable "tax checklist" on our site

3 Free "calculate your savings" calculators on our site

4 Partnerships with business attorneys and Chambers of Commerce (or other business groups)

5 Business Breakfast groups

6 Business Owners' Facebook groups

7 Tax tips columns, podcasts and radio

8 Pre-filing "bootcamps" to prepare for tax season

9 Specific "tips" newsletters to business
owners or other target market

10   "Brain Bootcamp" to train their
brainpower and bodies at the same
time.

If one of our markets for our oil-change service
is busy women, we can build an audience
through:

1 Partnerships with salons and dress shops

2 "Ladies' night" classes for women only

3 Car pickups from local businesses ("We'll
pick up your car and change the oil
while you're at the gym if you're on our
monthly subscription service")

4 Auto-email reminders every two months

5 Partnerships with local charities

6 Corporate plans (pick up cars from a local
business on a rotating schedule)

7 Partnerships with local car washes

There are several options for each, and there's
no reason a business owner can't pursue all of
them. In the "Awareness" stage, we can cast a

broad net. The only limitation: your first impression MUST create brand affinity. They have to like you right away.

How do you build an audience? You start with a gawker.

Following the Onboarding process laid out in this book, the first step to building an audience is simply to build awareness. Stand on a street corner; write a letter to the editor; place signage. Run free workouts in a park. Volunteer to cut kids' hair for free in the mall. Host a "CrossFit 101 Seminar" at a nutrition store. In short, start performing in a place your future clients visit.

Pay close attention to the first people to stand and watch: these are your gawkers. They'll explain what you're doing to everyone else; they might even be your first paying clients. For now, they're just paying attention, so give them as much as you can. Praise them. Know everything about them: their spouse's name, where they work, and what they do for fun. Repeat your message until the gawkers can do it for you.

You need someone else saying, "Hey, y'all! Come look at this!" That's your first gawker: a single onlooker SO awed, he'll tell a stranger. This is the tip of the spear.

The next step is to awe the second, third and fourth gawker. As a crowd gathers, the gawkers will educate them on what you're doing, and their message will ultimately determine the size of the crowd.

Nothing draws a crowd like a crowd does, but what KEEPS a crowd is a sticky story:
"He's on a hunger strike."
"He just woke up from a coma."
"He's going to jump!"
"He's about to propose to his girlfriend, up there in that window!"
"This guy is the next Jim Morrison!"

It's important for the early adopters, the gawkers who stand up close enough to smell you, to understand your message well enough to repeat it. Your most important messages should be condensed to their most important (and sticky) parts:

"Constantly-varied functional movement performed at high intensity."
"The cheapest airline in the southern States."
"The fastest tax returns available."
"The guy who will help you move if you buy a house from him."
"If you don't like it, it's free."

In Two-Brain Business, I wrote about "The Owner's Intent." These were one- or two-sentence "mission statements" to guide the team when the owner wasn't around. But in this case, our core message is designed to be shared, not used internally for making decisions.

What message will you pass to your gawker?
Here's the process:

1. What problem does your service solve?
2. How do you solve that problem better than anyone else?
3. What makes your service new or novel?
4. Why NOW?
5. Put those words into a sentence. That's your core message. Pass it to everyone.

If you're busking on a street corner, your core message might be: "I'll play any song for $2...but I'll play a Beatles song for $5!"

"I give free haircuts to any kid whose parent gets theirs done. They can even match!"

"I'll send you my free weight loss guide and exercise demos if you enter your email address below!"

The "Awareness" stage of Onboarding focuses your efforts on brand recognition. Get in front of gawkers and give them a replicable message. An audience starts with one person who wants to hear you play; the line forms behind them.

How Many Gawkers?

In The Technium, Kevin Kelly writes about "1000 True Fans." (http://kk.org/thetechnium/1000-true-fans/) He points to a very simple formula: 1000 fans, each paying $100 per year, creates $100,000 in annual revenue.

As more service providers attempt to "productize" their service by selling subscription models or selling a low-priced service to thousands of people, Kelly believes it's better for local service providers to focus on their "1000 True Fans" and make a decent, if not stellar, lifetime income.

This number--1000--is different for every industry, of course. Gyms (of which I'm an owner) can do well with 150 members if their average revenue per client is high enough. I lay out that process in two books, "Two-Brain Business" and "Two-Brain Business 2.0." In a service business, 1000 might be too few: for a hairdresser with an average cut price of $50, it will take 2000 clients to reach $100,000 in gross revenue.

Kelly's premise is really this: know your best clients. Make sure they know you. Give them a repeatable message that's different from everyone else. Then keep them in their seats.

Getting The Audience In Their Seats

The next stage in the Onboarding process is "Interest," sometimes called "Desire." If the Awareness stage is done well, the audience will be receptive to the music.
The help offered at the "Desire" stage should bridge the Awareness stage with the Integration stage. At the "Desire" stage, an audience is paying attention, but not yet paying money for your help. This is a bridge most potential clients will never cross: the market

reading your website and seeing your flyers is far larger than the audience who actually buys tickets. But a bit of work can improve those numbers.

Look at your daily website hits, and track first-time visitors: even if there are hundreds, less than 1% will take the next step. That's a remarkable opportunity, so I'll say it again: if you can make a clear and genuine offer to help at this stage, you'll do far better than any "get my name out there" advertising. These folks are already interested; just not interested ENOUGH. Yet.

Marketing in the "Interest" stage must demonstrate a solution to a problem. This can happen in two different ways: Conversation or Content. The latter will be covered extensively in the next section, but the Conversation should be broken down here.

Most of the time, a client's first encounter with our brand happens without our knowledge. A friend mentions your services at a party, or your building is part of the scenery on their commute. This is the first part of the conversation (Awareness.)

Some will follow their curiosity to your website or Facebook page or other media. These folks are looking for inspiration to action. They want you to make a case for using your business. But they're also looking for excuses: reasons to go somewhere else.

Opinion polarizes: a blog post on a political topic will impress 50% of U.S. voting citizens, but push the other 50% away. Religion will do the same, and maybe that's fine with you. It's all part of the conversation, just as it would be on a first date.

Just as on the first date, the conversation doesn't have to lead to a wedding proposal: it should just lead to a second date. That's important to keep in mind: I'm just as guilty as anyone of trying too hard to "sell" my services the first time I meet someone. I'm a raving CrossFit fan, and I'll talk to anyone about it. Whether in person or through email, the most important part of the "Desire" stage is to keep the conversation going until the client is ready to pay for your help. The process, in a nutshell, is this:

Help everyone you meet ->demonstrate how you can help more ->let them take action on trust.

If a client has indicated interest, your first priority should be to continue the conversation. In person, this is easy: "Can I call you later?" But digitally—where most conversations now start—it's critical to get the contact information of anyone who will provide it.

For example, if a client in my city wants to lose weight, they can visit a free Facebook page run by our gym. From there, they'll see a post to download a free weight loss guide from our site. To get the guide, all they need to do is enter their email address, and our system will automatically send an email containing a ton of information on weight loss. In fact, it's all the information they'll ever need to lose weight. But most will want MORE: knowing how to lose weight doesn't help most people actually lose weight.

To continue the conversation, we provide more information for free: every few weeks, we'll send an email with more weight-loss tips to everyone who downloaded our free guide. We'll include recipes, an exercise demo and some motivation in every email, and also a link to book a free one-on-one conversation with one of our experts.

Many times, these free conversations are between an expert coach and a fan who's been enjoying our free content for awhile. They know everything already: they just want to come in investigate. When they're sitting on a plyo box across from me, they don't need a sales pitch: they just need for me to smile and confirm what they already know. In other words, all I have to do is avoid giving them a reason NOT to sign up. For that reason, the client does most of the talking; it's the opposite of a sales pitch. My job is just to coach the client toward the best decision for them.

The most common question I hear during these meetings is, "What do you recommend for me?" They trust my expertise; they trust my intentions. And I don't let them down: I recommend the best service for them, regardless of the price. And 90% of the time, they buy it.

In my consulting business, I've done over 650 free calls (as of June 15, 2015.) These can last up to an hour, and they're done on my own dime. But I never have to "sell" anything. I've never had anyone ask for a discount.

Sometimes people are even surprised to hear from me personally, and not an assistant (this makes my wife laugh.)

As one example, I got an email last Wednesday at 5pm. Here's what it said:

"Chris, you don't know me, but I own a gym in (X.) We're in serious trouble. If things don't turn around in the next 90 days, I'll be bankrupt. I think you're the only one who can help."

Does this sound like someone who needs to be "sold" on our services? Luckily, a few weeks later, he's starting to turn the gym around. He stopped reading the "help wanted" ads every day, and his clients are happy to see the changes.

Another example from my own gym: a few months ago, I was walking to my truck after coaching my favorite class. It was a brilliant day, and I almost missed the man peering in the windows outside. I called to him by name, waved, and walked over.

He was surprised to be remembered. In 2006, he'd been a member of my cycling group, and I hadn't seen him since. But he'd been reading my newsletter every month for nine YEARS before coming back. It took that long before the stars aligned: his schedule matched mine, we were offering a service he found appealing, and he happened to be driving past the gym. We'd been having a conversation for almost a decade. We continued the conversation inside. The specific tactics (newsletters, landing pages, social media, etc.) are below. But let's talk through some conversations for other services:

Accountant:

Free "Health and Wealth" seminar with a local personal trainer -> email newsletters with helpful tips for investing every month, or "reminders" to contribute to savings plans before tax time -> information on a special 3-

year tax filing plan (33% discount for those who commit for 3 years?) ->clickable link to a calendar, where clients can book a free consultation ("Bring me your messy shoebox full of receipts!") ->client registration.

Hairdresser:

Free "Style Show" at a local fashion show fundraiser ->download a "how-to guide for hair accessories or quick "DIY" styles or "How To Keep Your Do" guide -> free consultation for a "special day" package or "Mother's Day Makeover" plan, with link to a booking calendar -> "thanks" email with recommendation for future purchases and link to booking calendar ->reminder to book recurring appointments to keep the fresh look.

Car Sales:

Free "Test Drive for Charity Day" ->capture email and send a "thanks for helping; here's 20% off your next oil change" coupon -> email link to schedule regular maintenance appointment ->helpful guides for new car shoppers ->invitation to a personally-selected test drive opportunity ("Hey Simon! I have this new car in, and I think you'd love it. Want to take it home overnight and take your kids out for ice cream?") -> an offer to let the client keep the car and their regular appointment schedule for one rate.

Massage Therapy:

Free "Partners Massage" or "Fix Your Athletic Problems" workshop->capture email and send newsletter on stretching, posture and mobility->add "when to call an expert" description to every "self-massage hack"->offer a free consultation link to calendar→encourage a regularly scheduled appointment to stay ahead of problems.

There are common steps to all service professionals. Every conversation starts by "Helping First." The next step is to know who you're helping (collecting info.) The third step is demonstrating expertise and continuing the conversation until the future client becomes a current client.

It's a simple process, and takes only six to ten

hours every month to execute. But it's the critical step most business owners try to skip by "selling" themselves on the first date.

Strategy: Establishing Authority

One of the largest branding strategies we teach is 'Establishing Expertise.'

It's a big one, operating on three levels, and is critical for both recruitment and retention.

In exit interviews, one of the most common reasons honest clients give for leaving is, "I wasn't learning anything anymore." What this really means is, "I don't think the coach had anything else to teach me."

What happens when an athlete believes they've learned all they can from you? They move on, or become a coach, or open their own box. There may be a lot MORE to learn…but they don't know what they don't know.

Tell them.

Start with 'why': why are we doing this workout? Why now? Why these exercises in this combination?

Then, 'how': how should this feel? How will it benefit ME, the client?

Instead of spending all your time on 'what,' start telling 'why' and 'how.'

Example:

"This workout will be tough. The alternating periods of work and rest will optimize your body's fat-burning response for the rest of the day."

"This workout will require all-out effort when you're already tired. You're a police officer, and you'll need to be ready to fight after chasing down the suspect."

"This haircut will keep you in style without being avant-garde. I want people talking about YOU, not your hair."

"I chose to show you this house because there's less traffic on this street. Your kids will only have to cross one intersection on the way to school, and they have a traffic guard who always shows up early. Her name is Pam."

"I'm going to massage your hip flexors to help your sore back. The hip flexor connects to your iliopsoas, which runs right through your pelvis and attaches to your psoas, where you're feeling the pain."

Your clients need to be reminded why they choose your service every time they see you.

"Always be closing" is just a funny preamble to a joke about selling steak knives, but you should always be HELPING as much as possible. "Help First" isn't complete without educating the client.

Building a "Community"

It's widely understood that the largest differentiator between box programs and 'other' fitness is the community of athletes. The Games help; Reebok helps; novelty helps; even satire helps. The community, though, is what changes lives.

In Dr. Allison Belger's "The Power of Community: CrossFit And The Force of Human Connection," the psychologist reinforces the idea that we are much greater than the sum of our parts. Sharing initiatives like Steve's Club, Dr. Belger explains how communities within Affiliates form the foundation on which great works can be performed. I can't recommend it highly enough.

As Dr. Belger illustrates, our generation has less involvement in social groups than any in recorded history. Raise your hand if you belong to the BPOE; the Shriners; the Legion; a knitters' circle, a reading group…even church attendance is at an all-time low. A box gym fills that social need – a critical level of Maslow's Hierarchy of Needs – for many of us.

Overtly, though, "community" is too abstract a concept for many.

In what is perhaps the greatest irony of the gym business, our greatest attribute is the one that carries the least promotional weight. It's too broad. "The community is awesome!" is both an understatement of truth and irrelevant to non-members. Social support isn't something you can advertise; people assume they already have enough friends.

Instead, 'Community' must be inferred; alluded to; pictured, but not billboarded.

The pictures, the causes, and the groups – they're all valuable for keeping people and creating a unified empathy. After they've signed up, 'community' is the flypaper…but it's not the fruit that got them there.

The 'bait' is Size Four. It's The Gun Show. It's the things with which your prospective new member is already familiar. It's framing the benefits of the programs against the backdrop of their current context. Talk about The Family to those already inside; talk about The Sweat to those at the door.

Brag about people who are just like your next client (you know what they look like, right? The NEXT guy? Can you sketch him with a pencil?) Tell stories about members. Take pictures of groups. Show the community, but sell the bikini.

Helping Strangers

When writing about audiences above, I included a section called "Getting The Audience In Their Seats." To sum up that section: show how your service solves their problem.

The best way to establish your authority and demonstrate your expertise is to create helpful content. Help the invisible stranger beyond the footlights, whose face you can't see but whose presence you feel.

When CrossFit.com launched in 2001, it presented a major challenge to a saturated market. The fitness industry was log jammed with the same old ideas. Coaches dangerously believed they knew all there was to know, and only novel gimmicks (balance balls, jiggling machines and jaw-biters at the time) were getting any attention. But CrossFit was completely different.

Instead of arguing about "fasted cardio" and the best body part splits, CrossFit pushed a lack of systemization. Workouts—posted every day on the site for free—seemed completely random. A daily "WOD" might include running, or climbing a rope, or pushing a sled, or throwing weight over your head…or all three, as fast as possible. It looked dangerous, and haphazard. To be completely honest, when I first heard about CrossFit in a triathlon transition area around 2004, I said, "that sounds like bullshit." Out loud. A decade later, I'm one of CrossFit's biggest proponents; I blog about the fitness, the business or the spirit every day.

What made people—the gawkers and early adopters, especially—read the website and try the workouts? Expertise.

CrossFit's founder, Greg Glassman, wrote about science every day. He was obviously an expert; he explained complicated concepts in a language everyone could understand. And though it was novel, his message made sense: life DOESN'T occur in sets and reps. We DON'T need more carbs; we need more balance. And practicing the habits of the best gymnasts, lifters and sprinters in the world will make us more fit. Treadmills, pec decks and leg extension machines will not.

The CrossFit Journal was published monthly back then, and it was 30-70 pages of high-quality, thought-provoking content. Though I subscribed to several professional Journals back then, every issue of CrossFit Journal contained something I could immediately use, with data to back up the ideas. Pictures showed impossibly-fit athletes doing impossible things. I couldn't wait to read more. For over a year, all I did was read.

Eventually, I became a CrossFit affiliate. I wrote about that process in "Two-Brain Business," so I won't repeat it here, but by 2012 I found myself working for CrossFit's media arm as a freelance content editor and writer. Still, I didn't understand the full power of education and authority until attending a CrossFit Media summit in San Francisco that year.

In a room with over 100 Media staff (the majority part-time content creators like myself,) then-Media Director Tony Budding reminded us: "We publish every day." I was astounded at the effort required (and given) to tell the stories of people doing CrossFit, and ways to exercise better. After all, there was no revenue model behind the content we were creating: it was all free, every day.

Today, if you visit the CrossFit.com site on Facebook, take a moment to look at its description: it labels itself a "media company," not a fitness company. As of this writing, there are over 13,000 CrossFit-licensed gyms worldwide, and Greg Glassman himself estimated over 500,000,000 CrossFit workouts would be done in 2015. Yes, the program works. But without education and authority, no one would ever know.

Content marketing is the best way to help a stranger, and it's the best way to grow your business. Content provides proof of your expertise; it provides emotional and logical reasons to use your service. In a world where any potential client can do unlimited research before buying, it's no longer enough to say, "I'm the best." Audiences need to be guided to their seats. And content marketing serves the role of usher.

So...What's Content?

Content is any educational work you create. It can be written (a blog,) spoken (a seminar,) recorded (a video) or dictated (a podcast.) It can be interactive, or pre-scripted. There's an entire industry set up to build marketing content. But you can do it entirely yourself.

If you're providing a service, you're an expert in your niche. You simply have to demonstrate that expertise through one of the media listed above.

For example, I coach business owners in the service industry (mostly fellow gym-owners.) My preferred medium is the written word, because I make a lot of mistakes and prefer to clean them up before anyone sees them. So I keep several blogs active, writing a minimum of 750 words per day (and up to 10,000 on some days.)

My blog topics are related to business, and I've done over 600 of them now. Every one seeks to solve one problem (only 10,000 problems left to solve!) for gym owners. When a gym owner has a particular problem, they can find some education on the topic at DontBuyAds.com or TwoBrainBusiness.com. If a gym owner has a problem and asks other owners for help (there are some huge Facebook groups for this purpose,) the others can share my posts. They frequently do.

In 2012, after posting 400 blogs on DontBuyAds.com, I compiled the best into a book called "Two-Brain Business." I was looking for a way to wrap up the blog before shutting it down.

But then I sold a few hundred copies. And then a few hundred more...ultimately reaching several thousand copies sold. Now I'm asked for autographs at seminars, and the phrase I hear most often on free consultation phone calls is, "I've read your book."

On our gym site, I post one motivational blog each week. We post one video demonstration every week as well, and tell the story of one client. Every Sunday, I publish the Catalyst Podcast, and our newsletter is greeted by over 3000 readers on the 20th of every month.

It sounds like a lot, I know. It probably sounds like more than you have time (or inclination) to do. But here's the good news:

- a LOT of this content is reusable.
- Most of it is just like having a conversation;
- finding topics is easy; and, my favorite:
- you don't have to make it all yourself.

For example, if you create a video to educate first-time homebuyers on "how to find problems before it's YOUR house," you can leverage that content on a website or newsletter for years. If you post pictures of new trends in fashion—or host a seminar on accessorizing—you'll gain local followers. If your newsletter gives a useful tax tip for small business owners every month, I'll read it.

The bottom line: potential clients are only "potential" because they haven't made the connection between your service and their problem.

When I record our weekly podcast, I simply flip on the mic and have a conversation with my coaches. Even my ten-year-old has a podcast (Avery's Books) to promote her website (averysbooks.com.) She sits on a couch in my office, strums her guitar a few times, and we talk about what she's reading and whether other kids might like it. Then she "interviews" her little brother on what HE'S reading—the same conversation we might have had later at the dinner table. It's relaxed, and she has a few hundred subscribers.

For blog post inspiration, I usually just write about my own challenges. Usually, after a missed lift attempt or faster 5k run, I'll be primed to write about something eating me up. But often I'll also find inspiration in audiobooks; I'll learn a new concept, consider how to apply it to one of my businesses, and spell it out for others in a blog post.

What REALLY burns you up? What mistakes are others making? What are the things you "vent" about? Clean up your language, make a logical point and use the opportunity to teach your audience. They don't want a rant, but they're starving for knowledge.

A final point: as I spell out in "Two-Brain Business 2.0," you don't have to develop all the content yourself. Your staff should establish THEIR expertise, too, and that means developing their OWN content.

In my gym, we have monthly coaches' meetings. The second item on the agenda is Continuing Education. Our Head Coach chooses a topic, and assigns us each some study help on the topic. Then we each share what we've learned through content we create. For example, next month's topic might be Weight Loss. The Head Coach says, "Here's what I want you to read and study. Who will write a blog post? Who wants to host a seminar? Who would rather shoot a video or do a podcast?"

We choose our assignments, and have 30 days to complete them. This produces up to 8 pieces of unique content every month.

Here's how to create a simple 300-word blog post:

FIRST PARAGRAPH

Explain how your topic will help the reader. Give them a reason to pay attention. Benefits, not features:

"Squatting will keep you out of the nursing home. It's the single most important exercise you can do. Here's how to do it right."

SECOND PARAGRAPH

Show, don't tell. Keep instructions simple, and use pictures to illustrate what you want.

"Push your hips back until your weight is on your heels (you should be able to wiggle your toes.)"

Focus on what to DO, not what to avoid.

THIRD PARAGRAPH

Give examples: when should people squat? How often?

"Try to do ten perfect squats in a row. Include squats in your warm-up, or do 20 while the coffee's brewing!"

FOURTH (SUMMARY) PARAGRAPH
Give the reader a "next step" to take.
"Click here to watch a video demo!"

Tactic: Instructional Videos

STEP ONE

Don't set up a sound stage: just coach a class as you normally would, and record the "skills" portion. Use your phone, a small video camera or DSLR. Record the whole thing.

STEP TWO

Review the video, and find the best cue or tip you used. Cut that portion and drop it into iMovie or Corel Video Studio Pro.

STEP THREE

Add your logo to the start and finish.

STEP FOUR (OPTIONAL):

Clean up the background noise. In iMovie, reducing background noise by 50-55% can remove hum without distorting your voice too much. Or use a more sophisticated tool like Audacity.

STEP FIVE:

Add a simple "next step" for viewers: a site to visit, a Facebook link, or another video to watch.

STEP SIX:

Post to your YouTube Channel. Add a link to sign up for your intro session in the video summary.

THIS IS IMPORTANT: Don't wait until you can create a perfect video. Consistency is better than perfect lighting and sound.

START HERE: Video the movements you teach in your OnRamp or Foundations program first. These are the most important, and most usable in future content marketing.

AND...ACTION!

Tactic: Event Photography and Photo Albums

In "Two-Brain Business," I wrote about The Yearbook Committee: clients with an artistic bent who love to take pictures, shoot video, or blog about their experience with you. These are folks who are passionate about the service you provide...but also passionate about their art. We can use their help, and they can use our podium to broadcast their art to a larger audience.

My friend Jeremy is a videographer. He does professional video production for real estate agents (www.rabbitview.com.) His videos sell houses. But he's also a wrestler, and loves to film wresting matches. His videos have been used to help kids get scholarships, to promote gyms and to teach skills. He does a lot of wrestling videos—for free—every year, because he loves it.

Tactic: Telling Client Stories

No one uses "testimonials" anymore. They're too staged, too sales-y. We've all been asked for a testimonial and recall how awkward it felt.

But we still need social proof to help our clients relate to our service. And our brains are wired to remember stories better than single concepts or facts. So tell stories on your site!

Client stories are sticky content. They make the featured client feel important. And they remind everyone else about how great about your gym "family."

Here's how to get three client stories every month with very little effort:

WRITTEN

It's important for a featured client to tell their story in their own words. Just prompt them with questions that lead to a narrative with a beginning, middle and end.

Email the following "interview" questions, with this lead:

"Hey Sara, it's fantastic having you in the gym. You bring so much to the noon group, and we want to make sure everyone knows your story. Can you answer these questions for us? Don't worry about your answers, and don't spend more than ten minutes. If you can send it back by Friday, we'll post it on Monday with some GREAT pictures of you working out!

1. What brought you to CrossFit in the first place?

2. What was your first impression? How has that changed?
3. What was your first "bright spot"?
4. What are you working on now?
5. What's your favorite Catalyst memory?"

Then find 2-3 great pictures of Sara. When she responds, cut the interview questions from her text so her post reads like a narrative. Paste to her blog; don't correct her language, but fix her grammar if necessary (always help your clients look their best.)

Post!

VIDEO

Ask a client if they can stay four minutes after class:

"Sara, we love having you here, and I want to make sure ALL of our clients know who you are. Can you stick around after class for a quick interview? I'll put it on our site next week."

Then prompt Sara with the same interview questions above. Keep the conversation rolling, and make it clear that her job isn't to sell your gym. Don't make it awkward. Smile while she's talking.

Drop the interview into iMovie.

IMPORTANT: It's better to be consistent (and have many) than to have high-quality "produced" videos. In fact, a client who is clearly speaking "off the cuff" about how much she loves your gym will be far more credible than a polished spokesperson.

REWARD: Thank your interviewees with a special "mango."

SAMPLES: Visit the Catalyst "client stories" area [link: http://catalystgym.com/client-stories/] for dozens of examples.

February 5, 2015 by

I came to CF because of a display Catalyst had at a Wellness Fair at Sault Area Hospital. I spoke to Jarrett there, and it sounded interesting, so I booked an appointment for my wife and I. We visited the gym and spoke to Melanie; I signed up for On Ramp and liked it, and went on from there.

I had been doing other things for exercise, such as yoga, cross country skiing, and cycling, but I had never really done much upper-body exercise, so the weight-lifting was new to me.

Quite frankly, the first impression was a bit intimidating, because the workouts are so strenuous, but that went away fairly quickly. The atmosphere created by the coaches and participants is encouraging, not pushy, so you quickly realize that the idea is to try hard and to improve your fitness, not to snatch 400 pounds.

The biggest improvement comes when you realize how much the workouts are about mind over matter. I was joking with Jess the other day when she described the Manmaker AMRAP WOD as "100% mental", but I knew what she meant. When I first started, early in many of the workouts I would start telling myself that I would never make it to the end. However, I always did make it to the end somehow, and eventually I quit sending myself the negative messages.

I never work on anything in particular, as I just attend the 0700 group three times a week

Tactic: Seminars

Engaging a client requires education and inspiration. But not necessarily at the same time.

The primary bridge between the "awareness" and "desire" stages is education. Namely, the knowledge convincing them your service will solve their problem. As the academic system is slowly realizing, we don't all learn the same way: some are more auditory, some more visual. Some are doers, some are memorizers. A variety of media is important for education.

An open invitation to the gym for a "seminar" instead of a workout can help potential exercisers cross the gap in their knowledge. As a species, we fear what we don't understand. Any path to understanding will help. And just as our client's motivation might be different from our own, their preferred method of acquiring knowledge might be different.

One example: I'm a writer. I love to read, and I type over 5000 words in the average day. But MOST visitors to my site would prefer video content over the long-form written word. And some would like to visit and chat, or watch me perform a bit before exercising with me.

Hosting a seminar on "What is CrossFit?" can be the bridge, or easy entry point for some who are disinclined to reading your blog every day. If they're interested enough to visit the gym and listen, they're only a short jump away from participation. The key is gaining permission to continue the conversation after the short seminar is over.

For instance, if we promote a 40-minute informational seminar on your service, and require preregistration, we can add each attendee's name to a newsletter list to send follow-up information:

"In this seminar, we'll provide our Top Ten Tax-Saving Tips of 2015. It's completely free, but space is limited: click here to reserve your spot!"

If you're not a public speaker, or run out of topics, you can "borrow" the expertise of another. A chiropractor can host a local Personal Trainer to speak about "First Steps Into Fitness," for example, and invite her clients to the event.

The Trainer will gain valuable access to a waiting audience. And the chiropractor will gain a link: if the seminar is posted on YouTube, it will create solid expertise content. When a local client does an online search for the Trainer, the chiropractor's name also appears on the video that pops up in the search results. In best cases, non-competing services with overlapping target markets can partner for seminars to gain access to the clients of the other. "Health and Wealth" seminars, between financial planners and personal trainers, are becoming more popular. Registration info can be gained by both parties, and audiences expanded quickly.

Newsletters are effective at every stage of the Onboarding process. They raise awareness when they're shared; they increase desire by demonstrating the benefits of our service. They provide a clear path to integration, and keep our existing clients engaged.

Newsletters follow a "good-better-best" delivery continuum:

Good: you send out a newsletter once every month with a good story.
Better: You send out one newsletter each month with a good story and an offer tweaked for different groups, and including a clear call to action.
Best: You send out multiple versions of the same email in a timely strategy (see below.) You include clear calls to action, and

demonstrate the benefits of your services. People look forward to receiving your newsletter.

Here's how to start with #1, and get to #3:

TITLE

Use "News" or "Stories" in the title. You're attracted to stories. Ask a question when possible: "Are You Wasting Your Time in the Gym?"

CONTENT - GENERAL

1. Client Story #1. Write a short intro paragraph: "I remember Carl's first day..." Post a great picture, and then link back to Carl's story on your site.
2. Offer #1. Make the offer relatable to the story: "Carl started with our new OnRamp program. Here's how:" Include a clickable link to sign up for OnRamp.

3. Client Story #2: Keep the reader scrolling down the page. Use the same format as Client Story #1.
4. Offer #2: Mention a service that existing clients might like, or list upcoming specialty groups and events. Include clear links to sign up.
5. Client Story #3: Follow the same format as above.
6. Personal note: though all of the above should be written in professional language (third-person, active tense) this section should be in the first-person and typed the way you speak.

The 'General' newsletter will go out to everyone on your list that isn't in a "special interest" group. For those folks, you'll edit the original email to include relevant content for them.

CONTENT – PARENTS OF KIDS WHO PLAY SPORTS (example)

1. Client Story #1. Use a kid from your CFK program ONLY if you have express permission to do so. Make sure you have a photo release on your waiver, but ask their parent if you can feature them. If not, use the same client story from your GENERAL newsletter.
2. Offer #1: explain the BENEFITS of your CFK program (or sport-specific training program.)
3. Education #1: Parents need reassurance that your program is: a) safe; b) a good fit for their schedule (relevant); and c) fun for their kid. Link to CFJ articles with a one-paragraph lead-in. Even better: write blog posts about youth training, and link to those.

NEWSLETTER FREQUENCY

Debate rages about how often to send your newsletter, but I prefer this schedule:

Tuesday morning (around the 20th of the month) at 10am. This provides enough time for clients to check their schedule for next month, but not enough time to forget to register (a bit of urgency.) Inboxes are jammed on Mondays, but readers' brains are still fairly fresh on Tuesdays, and they're likely taking a break around 10am.

You use different versions for different interest groups (i.e. Weight Loss, Sports Performance, Parents, etc.)

DETAILS

Include "unsubscribe" links. Readers who 'unsubscribe' can always subscribe again later, but people who hit "spam" will probably never get your emails again, even when they're ready for them. Use the "Check for Spam" option to see the likelihood of your email being bounced. Include only one or two pictures, since many servers will filter out emails with large attachments. MailChimp and Constant Contact will usually prompt you to do these automatically.

IMPORTANT:

The best software won't work unless you USE it with consistently good content. Many clients pay hundreds each month for software like Aweber or Infusionsoft, but fail to use the software at a level that will give them any return on their investment.

Also, don't spam people. "Drip" campaigns make me shudder. What's YOUR first reaction when you get an unsolicited email? How about one that doesn't give you anything of value, but tries to sell you on a service?

Tactic: Podcasts

The key challenge with using content marketing is gaining and keeping the audience's attention. Most content online is consumed in a passive state—the reader or watcher has to be sitting down facing a screen. This is not the case with a podcast: its greatest strength is its ability to be consumed while doing other things.

Podcasts are better than radio shows while driving. They're better than most music while working out. They're bite-sized pieces of education that are consumable while walking your dog.

Podcasts are very easy to create using management portals like BuzzFeed, which I use for the Catalyst Podcast, the Enrichment and Education podcast, Two-Brain Radio (my business podcast,) and my daughter's weekly show about books she's reading (Averysbooks.com.)

When recording, I simply have the same conversation I'd normally have with one of my coaches, with a small difference: the mic is on. I ask them questions about our gym's programming, or new research on weight loss, or lifting techniques, and record the whole thing. Then I use free software like Audacity to edit out the boring stuff, paste in a little opening/closing riff, and publish.

Moments later, every subscriber to the podcast has my new "show" downloaded to their device automatically.

Podcasts currently have a much higher "open" rate than newsletters, because they're passive: when one podcast ends, the next begins automatically. As long as I'm delivering valuable, helpful content—I'm Helping First—it doesn't sound like a sales pitch for my programs. And they help with establishing context with the clients: hearing my voice is different than reading my words. If I take a picture of myself with the coach, I can use the picture (or a short video) to promote the podcast. As my audience grows, iTunes and Stitcher will even help me reach more local people.

Finally, I can help overlapping audiences by "interviewing" other professionals on my show. Extending the "health and wealth" idea above, I can invite a financial planner to be a guest on my podcast, and then give her links to share on social media with HER audience. This doubles my reach and exposes me to an overlapping target market: those in my preferred age demographic with disposable income and some thought to their future.

Tactic: Landing Pages

Landing pages on your website are like "side doors" to your business.

In one of the first sections of this book, I asked, "What DON'T your clients want?" and covered some more general points. But there are also elements on your website some clients shouldn't see, or should see only when they're ready.

For example, if a financial brokerage sells mortgages, 401k plans, index funds and life insurance, the sheer volume of information might be overwhelming. When dealing with money, clients can easily suffer "paralysis by analysis," in which their minds are so boggled by math and fear they wind up taking no action at all.

Instead, if the brokerage sets up a landing page for mortgages, a client searching for mortgages in their city can "land" on a section of the site that's most relevant. Later, they might return to the same brokerage for guidance on life insurance; but for now, decisions should be simple and help the client find what they want.

At my gym, we train elite athletes and regular folks; skinny people, and severely overweight people; barbell warriors ("firebreathers") and timid introverts. A strong mix is good for everyone, and we have solid systems for retention after they've joined. But that doesn't mean a weight-loss client wants to see a video with loud rap music highlighting a man-beast collapsed on the floor, trying not to pass out after a crazy workout. Likewise, the teenage football player doesn't want to read about setting small goals in order to lose weight. Each potential client finds his way to you through a different path. When they're seriously considering your service, it's crucial to have the right message reach them at the right time.

When someone searches for "Weight Loss in Coopersville" (not my real city,) I want her to go straight to a page for weight loss information on my site. I don't want them to have to navigate around links for Sports Performance or CrossFit or Yoga; I want the information right in front of them. In time, they'll be introduced to CrossFit. But a weight loss client might not KNOW CrossFit is the best way to lose weight until I explain it to them. The landing page is where the explanation begins; it bridges the gap, or at least brings them through the door.

We run a huge program for kids and teens, and though we call it CrossFit Kids, the program isn't just a watered-down version of CrossFit. It's a completely different focus on skill acquisition and body awareness instead of high-intensity weightlifting and interval training. Parents visiting my site should be guided first to information about building well-rounded athletes; fun workouts that kids enjoy; and safe resistance training. After we set the context (balance, fun, safety) we can introduce the CrossFit Kids methodology without putting a nervous parent on edge.

The other purpose of a landing page is to collect information and continue a conversation. The collection of information can be a tradeoff, so many businesses will offer long-form, downloadable content on their site in exchange for an email address. Then the reader's address is added to a newsletter list that will send them more helpful content over time.

For example, in December 2014 I was speaking at a local electrical company about nutrition. One parent recognized me as a coach in a game against her son's team the previous weekend. When she asked how our team had so much energy at 7am, I told her the parents deserved the credit. All I'd done, I said, was given them a short little guide on how to feed their kids (and get them to eat before an early game.)

"How can I get a copy of that?" she asked.

I offered to send the eating guide to anyone who wanted a copy. A dozen hands shot up, and I collected their email addresses.

That afternoon, after cleaning up my document a bit, I sent it out to each parent. Then I realized how many parents might want the same information: literally hundreds in our hockey-crazy town. So I built a landing page called, "How To Feed A Hockey Animal," added a picture of my own hockey-crazy son eating cake in his goalie equipment, and offered the three-page guide to anyone who wanted it.

If a parent wanted to read the guide, they simply had to enter their email address on a form in the page, and my email software would automatically send the guide their way. Later, I began sending helpful information relevant to parents of athletes to each address every month. There were articles on concussion, resistance training, and burnout in sports—all high-quality content that was relevant to this list of parents. Within three months, our teen program had a waiting list. Eight months later, we've doubled the number of classes for teens—and we still have a waiting list.

The key to gathering contact information is QUALITY content that's RELEVANT to the audience. No one wants to buy a ticket for a Jazz festival and hear symphony music. And no one wants to download the Philharmonic, only to find they've purchased thrash metal by accident.

Some other examples:

We have weight loss guides, "how to squat" videos, "Fit The Dress" Guides (for brides,) nutrition tracking booklets, concussion symptom checklists and all sorts of other content on our gym website. You won't see them if you go to the front page, but if you search for a specific keyword, you'll be led straight to them.

Landing pages bridge the Awareness and Desire stages by teaching your future clients how you'll solve their problem.

If I owned a shoe store, I'd produce videos and articles explaining how to match shoes to dresses. I'd educate my future clients on style, fit and durability. If anyone searched "wedding dress in Coopersville" in my town, they'd be led right to my "How To Buy A Dress: Think With Your Feet" page.

If I were selling wine, I'd produce videos every week matching wines with different foods. I'd explain how wine is graded, and how to buy a great wine for $20. Gary Vaynerchuk was on to this idea almost 15 years ago, before social media was around. Today, thanks to this same tactic, he's an internationally renowned marketing superstar. It's not the tactics that are important, but the intent: if you're looking for the best way to HELP, instead of the best way to SELL, you'll find both.

Tactic: "Podiums"

Every client is a psychological client.

What's stopping your clients from walking into your shop to get their teeth cleaned? Why won't an overweight man lose weight? Why won't the busy professional woman hire a housekeeper?

They're scared. Scared you'll say they have bad breath. Scared you'll laugh when he can't do a squat. Scared her house isn't clean enough to let the housekeeper see it.

What will get them over the hurdle? Motivation, of course. But although we know motivation is necessary for long-term success, few people—even in my industry—realize success is necessary for motivation.

Clients need to "win." Your service helps them solve a problem—otherwise known as WINNING.

Hair game on point? You WIN.

Dress fits like a glove? You WIN.

Getting a tax refund? You WIN.

What happens when you win at the Olympics? You stand on a podium, get your picture in the papers and on cereal boxes. You're asked to advocate for different products that helped you get there. People want to read your story. You're famous.

What happens when your braces come off? Well…maybe you get popcorn and chew gum.

What happens when you lose weight? What happens when you stop having back pain? What happens when you're promoted? Nothing quite as good, I promise. You might celebrate in public, but no one's holding a parade. No one is putting you on the podium you deserve. Your clients deserve a podium. They deserve a "win" once in awhile.

What if kids had their picture taken and shared on Facebook when their braces came off? What if a client who did their first 5k showed up in the paper, beaming at the finish line? What if every client to receive a tax refund had their picture taken with a check, and appeared on your podcast and website?

What if they got to PICK their own podium? What if, at the start of a workout, a client was asked, "What will make you happy here? What will make you proud?" Or instead of a toy, a nervous little boy in a dentist's chair was asked what behavior would make him proud while his teeth were checked? If he says, "I won't be scared," and then makes it through his checkup, he'd probably rather see his picture on the wall than get a lollipop. It's human nature. Every client is a psych client.

Celebrating the success of your current clients can help future clients make the connection:

"That guy did it. So can I."

"That woman found a dress to fit her, and she's larger than I am."

"That guy lost weight, and he's even older than me!"

"That woman's teeth were stained worse than mine from coffee—and now they look great! There's hope for my teeth, too."

This is called, "Social Proof," and it's part of our human makeup: when we see other people doing things, we ask ourselves what it would be like to do the same. We try on their shoes. We "ooh" and "aah" at the tightrope walker because we're imagining ourselves on the high wire. Show success: great haircuts, fabulous-looking dresses, weight-loss triumphs.

One of the greatest tactics is simply to "tell the story of people using your service." How did your dress make the teen's prom a success? How did your bookkeeping save that man's business? It's not bragging: it's inspiring necessary action by others. It's coaching others to do what they know they should. It's helping. One of the tactics above, "Mavens," lays out a very simple way to do this on a consistent basis every month. Celebrate success: give people podiums.

Building A Robust Marketing Strategy

What killed Sears?

Sears used to be a retail giant. Its story is compelling: when a shipment of watches was accidentally delivered to a railway worker in the 1880s, Richard Warren Sears sold them up and down the line. Within a few years, he was running a mail-order company so huge he had to invent the assembly line (though Henry Ford was given credit.) Within fifty years, his named adorned the tallest tower in the world.

But then the fall started: price competition, a less-loyal customer base, and smaller margins forced Sears into a gradual decline. When Wal-Mart surpassed Sears as the largest volume retailer in the U.S. in 1989, its vice presidents blamed "unfair" price practices. It crashed hard: within ten years, its credit company was purchased by Citibank, its stores repurposed and catalogs sent to the shredder. The brand was purchased by Kmart in 2004.

What killed Sears wasn't its margins--one sale at Sears would net the company at least 12x the profit as a sale at WalMart--but its inconsistency in marketing.

Sears introduced the scariest rollercoaster in the world: the Sale flyer.

When Sears opened its first retail stores (just counters in warehouses, much like our gyms) it was competing only for attention with general stores. But as other "department" stores opened, it began to compete on price. The solution: short-term price adjustments to increase volume sales and "win customer loyalty."

And so the annual mail-order catalog was supplemented by the Winter Sales flyer. And Sears WOULD see a large spike in sales, though short-term. So the Winter Sales Flyer was quickly followed by the Summer Sales Flyer, and soon there was a Sale! Sale! Sale! sign all the time.

The problem was that customers stopped buying between sales. And that was very, very bad.

So Sears began to sell nearly everything "on sale," nearly all the time. When I was selling treadmills against them, I used to tell the story of the Sears Tire Sale to underline their shadiness. And client behavior was reinforced: they'd just wait for the sale, and then buy from Sears...unless another offer came along first, and it almost always did.

This marketing roller coaster is dangerous. Often, service businesses only think about "marketing" when cash flow dips. So they'll call their local radio station or newspaper and buy ad space. "You have to spend money to make money," they'll say. And their clients become conditioned to wait for sales or special offers. This is what made advertisers like Groupon popular: they're just a "Sale!" flyer for service businesses. And they've already caused a lot of damage.

Promotion itself isn't a bad thing. After all, if you don't tell people your story, no one else will. But marketing is a lot like your health: doing the right things all the time is preventative. Taking a big dose of medicine when you're in pain might help the symptoms...but not for long. And over time, you'll become immune to its benefits.

Rather than create huge peaks of promotion and valleys of low cash flow, we want a constant trickle of focused effort. Rather than gain ten new clients from our annual "bring a friend for FREE!" day, we want one new client from our website, one from a client referral, one from another business' referral, one from our facebook page...and we want each of those every month, please.

We want a marketing strategy, not just an advertising campaign. We want a steady drizzle, not a system of flood and drought.

As I wrote in "Two-Brain Business," consistency is more important than perfection. It can be hard to ignore the "flash-bang!" marketing hijinks that some advertisers advocate. In the early 1990s, "Guerrilla Marketing" was the most popular series of marketing books sold, because it was so different from the norm. Its author, Jay Conrad Levinson, told stories of staged car crashes and tanks driving through Times Square. These were shock-and-awe attention-getters, and they worked.

But in marketing, ten years might as well be a hundred. Now EVERYTHING is a shock-and-awe attention-getter, and we're competing for that attention long before we compete for money. Car crashes are everywhere. Single-impression advertising, even when involving surprise, simply doesn't work for long.

Part of the reason is the rise of cell phones. When you take a picture of something you see, you're less likely to recall the details later. You don't have to: the camera holds the memory for you. So your brain prioritizes other information. To be remembered, a story must be told in a memorable way, and that takes time.

Single-occurrence events can be part of a larger story, but can no longer be the entire tale. We want to know WHY the car crashed, and what happened to the victims, and whether it's likely to happen to us. In short, we want a beginning, a middle and an end: all the parts of a good story. And we want new stories all the time. This leads us back to consistency.

This book will reveal several marketing strategies, not just advertising campaigns. All are long-term. All will snowball if you keep pushing them. Some are more appropriate for you right now; some will become more appropriate for you later. The important thing is to start right away, and consistently deliver on each one.

In the next chapter, you'll find a "Brand Action" chart. This chart is to help you build consistency. You'll slowly grow to delivering on many marketing strategies at once.

To start, though, I'll break each down individually. I suggest careful consideration and practice on each before moving on to the next. Start one snowball, get it turning, then start the next. If you struggle to keep one moving, don't start another; wait until the first marketing strategy is so ingrained that you can do it without thinking about it. If you don't have time or inclination, have someone else do it and measure their success instead. It will get easier as you go.

When you learned to walk, you fell down a lot. But the first time you took two consecutive steps, your parents probably went nuts: it was a new trick in your portfolio. A big one.
A few weeks later, walking was a skill: you could do it consistently and on demand. You probably still fell down occasionally, but it no longer fazed you: it was just part of walking.
By eighteen months, you were walking up and down ramps, balancing on one foot, going backward. It was ingrained; it was just something you did. No more thought required. The progression from fluency to consistency to intensity isn't limited to fitness.
Learning to speak Spanish is the same: practice the basic nouns; put sentences together frequently; go to Spain. It's the same

with muscle-ups, handstand walking, and your business.

At our seminar, you'll hear this phrase: plan the work, and work the plan.

Planning the work with a mentor is a necessary first step.

But success over the long term means consistent application until execution is automatic.

For example, your first video teaching the squat is a trick. You have 30 outtakes, a choppy title sequence, and bad sound–but you did it: you have content. It's a big day. As you get better, the content improves and attention increases. Good for you: you're marketing. You can produce a video on muscle-up progressions on demand. Eventually, you get a GoPro and start shooting pistol progressions in Spain…

We're all looking for a 'trick.'

But the secret isn't one simple thing: it's consistency, then intensity. It's planning the work, and working the plan until it becomes automatic. Your first blog post won't be easy; the hundredth will be. Become skilled.

Tracking The Onboarding Process

How do you know your arms are weak?
You test them. You try pull-ups; you try pushups. You bend and flex your elbow while holding different weights. You record which lifts are easy, which are hard, and the weights and reps for each.
After a month of trying various lifts, you try each again—and, magic! Merely the act of trying the lifts has made you stronger at each! Testing yourself is training yourself. But if you don't write down your successes, you won't reach any "bright spots" in strength training, because you won't KNOW them. You won't be able to compare yourself against your former self, or your peers, or the world champions. How do you know your audience is finding your service, desiring your service, integrating smoothly into your service and sticking around long enough to reap the benefits? You track

them. You record every name at every stage, to start.

Here's a sample chart my mentoring clients use to track their Onboarding:

	Awareness			Desire			Integration				Retention		Cancelled memberships
	New FB Likes	Pixel Hits	Downloads	Newsletter Signups	No-Sweat Intros	Free Trial Class	OnRamp Packages	PT Packages Purchased	New Members	Specialty Group	Joy Girl Gift Recipients	Joy Girl MIA Calls	Cancelled Memberships
January													

Tracking In the Attention Stage

Ten years ago, it was very hard to see your audience. Until one walked past the stage lights and introduced himself, it was almost impossible to know who was out there watching.

Now it's much easier. In the "Awareness" tracking columns, we list attendees at our seminars; new "likes" on our Facebook page; signees in our guestbook at events; and ballots from our booth at other events. We trade free value in exchange for the right to call people back.

There are other ways: as social media becomes better at integration and different platforms share "cookies," we can see the websites visited by your clients before and after yours. The Facebook remarketing pixel "sees" Facebook users when they're on your site, and you can choose to advertise only to them later. Google Analytics can give you demographic information, time spent on each of your pages, and which pages are visited (in each order.)

In person, it's much tougher to get a potential client's contact information, so we trade a potentially valuable service. We attend trade shows and street fairs as often as possible, and never forget our "Prize" box.

When passersby stop and look at our sign, they're often waiting for an invitation to chat. We talk about the weather, answer questions about our service—but never try to sell anything. Instead, we invite them to fill out a ballot for a free week at the gym.

This information is later entered into our database, and the new client receives an auto-email the following day:

"Thanks for stopping by our booth yesterday. It was great to meet you. The winner of our 1-Week Free draw is Harry Reamus!

BUT for supporting our cause (Nurses' Week, or Family Day at the Park) we're offering you 50% off OnRamp if you sign up by Friday. Thanks again for helping a worthy cause!"

Free seminars and charity events are linked through the partner's website, and we always require pre-registration.

For example, if a car dealership was hosting a "Test Drive for Charity," they can capture the information of everyone who takes a test drive. Then they can email everyone the next day to thank them for supporting the event, and let them know how much was raised (a Bright Spot.) From there, the dealership can begin to establish their expertise with high-value information, like a used car buyers' guide. A relationship that starts from a foundation of "Help First" and moves toward Trust will be long-standing and profitable for everyone involved.

The key: look for opportunities to track everyone you meet.

When the audience is paying attention—but before they're paying you money—it's important to know what they want. After all, if you KNOW their problem, you can easily outline a solution. If you DON'T know their problem, you'll struggle to present solutions they care about. Try selling fat loss to a football player, for example, and they'll stop paying attention quickly.

We try to filter our target markets whenever possible.

Over the phone, it's easy to ask, "How did you hear about us?"

When a client walks in for the first time, their information should be captured. We ask walk-ins to fill out a waiver so we're ready when they come back. If every staff member is busy with other clients, the visitor can be guided to a guestbook.

We use an iPad for this purpose. Upon entry, if the office is empty, the iPad screen is set up to draw the eye. The screen rotates through a slideshow of happy Catalyst clients doing happy Catalyst things, and on top the text reads, "Sorry we're not here. Come and watch us in action, or tap the screen and we'll call you back right away."

If they tap the screen, they can enter their name and email address (our booking and billing software sets this up for us.) If they poke their head into the main gym area, they'll be spotted and greeted, and the coach will dash over to get them started on the Guestbook.

You can also use metadata: which pages on your website get the most hits? Which newsletter made the phone ring? Which street sign had people texting for more information? Email and Facebook messages provide better data about the sender, but allowing them to find their preferred service is the role of Landing Pages.

For example, if a client can visit your website, enter their information and download a "DIY Guide for Incorporating Your First Business," you'll know they're an aspiring entrepreneur. From there, you can congratulate them on taking the first steps and then send them helpful information to get them started. Your bookkeeping service will fit naturally into their plans—especially if they're using your free downloadable Cash Flow Calculator.

In the "Desire" columns, record every phone call, email, newsletter subscription, page form or ad respondent. Break them down, name by name, to see what's working over time.

Tracking In the Integration Stage

This is easiest: write down the name of everyone who pays you.

Integration is the period where clients make a decision: to buy, or to wait. When they accept your help, it's important to know why.

What brought them in the door? How did they first hear about the business? Walk them back in time. Record their answers. These are very important, because they tell you what's working, and how fast. How long does your Onboarding process take, on average? Is it days, or months? That's good information to have.

Pinpointing the successes is especially critical because it's hard to pinpoint the failures, as you'll read in the next section.

Tracking In the Retention Stage

Using the "Bright Spots" protocol, clients are called more often when they're new to the service. New clients require more frequent positive feedback, naturally. So at the gym, they're called after every new personal best. If they go missing, they're called and reminded of their goals.

In many cases, my preferred form of communication isn't shared by the client. Some people prefer text messages, for example. In those cases, I send a simple video of me, standing in front of a whiteboard with their name and a few of their goals written on it.

"Hey Tommy! Just wanted to chat with you about some of the goals you set. Just send me back a text to let me know when we can chat!" The most important part of tracking is to find out what's working. When a client has been absent from the gym for two weeks or more, it's tough to reboot their habit. In that case, a 50% return rate is a big win. Unless they're injured or travelling, a two-week workout break usually leads to a cancelled membership. Other service professionals can set their own timelines for follow-up. Financial planners might aim for an annual update; hairdressers should send out regular reminders. My kids' dentist calls them a week before their appointments. It helps with adherence AND long-term retention.

Complete neglect shows a client you don't care. If a client leaves because they "feel like a number," and you don't call them, you've proven them right.

Watching Trends in OnBoarding

Recording numbers at each stage is helpful. For example, if we track 50 people in the Awareness stage in June, but notice only one called our business for a consultation, we know there's a barrier between Attention and Desire. A growing audience is becoming aware of your brand, but doesn't understand how you can solve their problem. That leaves a clue: you need more content marketing (see "Getting The Audience In Their Seats.") Likewise, if you notice 10 new people signing up in June, but 9 cancelling their memberships or appointments, you have a retention problem. Fix this with a system like "Bright Spots." Do that first, so you're not always fighting for the NEXT clients instead of taking better care of your CURRENT clients.

Tracking OnBoarding success is good. Using numbers is good. But using names is better. Using names instead of just numbers allows us to see the flow of clients through our business. In the chart above, you could follow George Smith from Awareness (he attended a seminar) to Desire (he signed up for the newsletter) to integration (he bought Personal Training sessions.) George's progress provides clues, or OnBoarding Bright Spots: we know the seminar is successful at starting the conversation and moving the audience toward their seats. We know the newsletter is successful at moving the audience toward booking a consultation, at least. And we know our No-Sweat Intro can guide clients toward Personal Training.

If, by contrast, George came in for a free consultation and DIDN'T sign up, we know our intake process needs some work.

We can use this information to guide future "Help First" marketing, or refining our systems. Knowing that seminar attendees tend to sign up for the newsletter is important, because you can guide your seminar talk toward the newsletter. If we notice this trend instead: Visitors to our booth at the Beauty Expo→facebook page "likes"→free beauty tips page visits→purchase of the basic package→upgrade/retention

… we can make sure our banners and handouts clearly link to our Facebook page. Some clients will try harder to find more information; some will guide themselves through the OnBoarding process. By following their trail, we can guide others through the same process. When you find what works, put some muscle behind it. But if you're not writing it down every month, you'll never know where to focus your effort.

Over time, this tracking tool becomes more robust (and more valuable.) Trends will become clearer, efforts will prove or disprove themselves. There's no longer a need to guess whether any branding initiative is successful: either an idea moves people along in the Onboarding process, or it doesn't. If a seminar fails to capture the contact info of its attendees, or move them toward Desire, it should be rebuilt. If the newsletter, website or podcast doesn't increase walk-in traffic, phone calls or emails, it's not working. There's a barrier somewhere, and the OnBoarding Chart will shine a bright light at the sticking point.

In December 2014, I faced a conundrum: we were putting out great content in the form of blog posts and demo videos. Our corporate marketing was on point, and our Cobranding was strong. Our website hits were high; our open rates for newsletters were great. New landing pages were attracting new audiences, and our social media channels were exploding. But the phone wasn't ringing. We didn't have a single No-Sweat Intro scheduled in the first ten days. It wasn't a No-Sweat start to the month for me! But instead of throwing up my hands or bouncing my forehead off the drywall, the problem became a puzzle to solve. And OnBoarding showed the full picture: despite a ton of growth in the Awareness stage, and a slow rampup of client Desire, no one was taking the next step. What was the barrier to Integration? I wondered.

I looked carefully at my tools, and noticed a large commonality: a complete lack of Calls to Action. Blog posts ended without a link to click; videos were posted without a clear "next step" for viewers to take. I was guiding dozens of people toward dead-end roads.

Luckily, my content was engaging enough to keep viewers in the conversation. I added these links and registration forms to our new content, and removed the plug in the line. We broke a seven-day sales record in the first week of January. Every new client had been sitting in our OnBoarding funnel, waiting for me to tell them what to do next. Identifying the true problem and solving the puzzle resulted in tens of thousands of new revenue immediately. Advertising doesn't provide this opportunity. If a potential client sees an ad, or reads a flyer about your service, you might capture their attention for a fleeting instant. Taking the jump from Awareness to Integration is rare, but a tiny fraction of your audience WILL take that jump…if you show them how. Building a conversation, though, will keep them in the Desire stage longer, providing multiple chances to move them toward Integration.

In a perfect world, clients would flow through the OnBoarding process seamlessly. But in reality, clients wait.

They wait for the right time; the right offer. They wait for their schedules to clear. They wait for a raise. And they wait for a REASON. A deadline solves most of these problems. Sometimes the best help you can give a person it to ask, "Are you in, or are you out?"

In an earlier section, I wrote about how the "maybes" can kill you. But "maybe" also hurts the client; the sooner they get started, the more they can benefit from your service. Paralysis by analysis is very real.

If Las Vegas allowed gamblers to hem and haw at the tables, their profits would be cut in half. When one player calls, the rest show their hands immediately.

Time to call. In, or out?

At each stage in the OnBoarding process, we can help the audience make a decision with a Call to Action. These include deadlines ("Register before May 20!") attendance caps ("limited to the first 30 buyers!") or simply bonuses ("Sign up before June 1, and you'll get a free wax with your nails!")

A deadline is important. The next step is to create the shortest path to action possible. Ordering from Amazon used to take three clicks: one to add the order to your cart; one to take your cart to checkout; one to pay. But after tracking tens of thousands of abandoned virtual shopping carts, the team at Amazon worked hard to simplify the checkout process. "In, or out?" they asked their customers. And without the extra step, more customers answered, "In."

Most of our branding leads to one step: booking a free consultation, or "No-Sweat Intro." In, or out?

In some cases, we use landing pages to direct a special client away from the usual path and toward a different entry point. For example, if a client wants to sign up for a sport-specific training program (like basketball,) they can do so without a consultation because they have a specific performance goal in mind; they already know what they want. In those cases, we're best to simply get out of the way and allow the client to sign up for what they want. They bypass the usual route.

But 90% of our OnBoarding process leads to "Click Here To Book A Free Consultation." At that point, the client can choose any convenient appointment time through our online scheduler. We do this online for three reasons:

1. It's easier to click one more link than to pick up the phone. A client can maintain a low profile in the hierarchy of communication.

2. My staff doesn't have to answer the phone. If a potential client calls and doesn't receive an answer, they might wait for another day. And that "other day" might be in 2019.

3. Signing up for a fitness program is an emotional decision. These decisions aren't usually made at 8am, on a full stomach and optimistic mind. They're usually made at 10pm after a date with Ben and Jerry. When they reach an

emotional point of no return, I want to be ready to help immediately.

It's also important for clients to flow back and forth in the Onboarding process easily. "In, or out?" might be a bit misleading in this context; I never want a client to think "Now or never," but instead "Now! Now! Now!...but if not now, next week."

When a potential client needs help but can't afford the service today, they should stay engaged until their need exceeds their current priorities. If they fall off for awhile, the conversation can continue through your social media and other content until they're enticed to rejoin.

Creating Calls to Action

A sense of urgency might be the "tipping point" for a client when they're seeking help. Many folks wait until it's too late to ask for help; showing them how close they are to "too late" might help them make a quicker decision. Salesmen are trained to use closing techniques to speed up the sales process and force the client to take action. They'll create

"limited time offers" or "today-only discounts."
There are more closing techniques than I can
list in this book.

But in the service industry, a discount erodes
your most important asset: your time. Why
work just as hard for less money? Instead of
discounts, add sample services that will help
the client get further ahead.

For example, if a client books their wedding
party at your salon before May 1, they might
get a bonus limousine rental thrown in. Or
perhaps the local U-Brew Win Bottler offers
them a discount on their wine. This doesn't
devalue the service provider's time; helps the
client; and helps the OTHER service provider
gain a new client.

Consistent Delivery and "Shipping"

Plan the Work, Work the Plan.
Ideas are great. So are opinions. But action
makes success.

The best-laid plans won't do anything by
themselves. As I wrote in "Scientists vs.
Technicians" in 2011, some of the best thinkers
aren't the best at execution. Many gym owners
fall into this category: they have great ideas,
but never follow through, telling themselves
they don't have the time or resources.

To be most efficient at anything, you must
record the process and then strip away the fat.
You have to plan the work. Then you have to
execute: make a list, and go. Take action. Don't
be paralyzed by analysis.

Our Brand Action Plan is our monthly

marketing checklist. Readers of the TwoBrain blog will recognize many of the strategies; mentoring clients will already know exactly how to execute each one. This is how we consolidate our Branding Actions every month at Catalyst.

We try to achieve three Actions in each category. For example, we send three Corporate Intro Letters every month, prioritizing those companies at which our clients work. We set specific dates for "Bring-A-Buddy" workouts every month to create a sense of urgency. And we publish a LOT of content to establish authority. They're all different tactics under the "Help First" strategy.

The key, of course, isn't each individual tactic. It's the execution of all, done every month, year after year. Yes, we add new tactics all the time; this sheet allows us to fit those ideas into our overall plan for amplification.

	A	B	C	D	E	F	G	H	I	J
1	Month	Corporate intros sent	#igotthis	maven connection	service industry referrals	content published	newsletters sent	bring-a-buddy	special referral	special event
2	Jan						Fat Loss			
3	2015						Get Fit			
4							General			
5							Hockey Parents			
6	Jan									
7										
8										
9										
10										
11	Feb									Fit It Forward
12										
13										
14										
15										

Plan the work in advance, and ship on time.

A quick review on several of the strategies covered in this chart:

Corporate Introductions are the process of offering our service to a large corporation. Our goal is to help their employees, so we want a company employing more than a dozen people.

What does a corporation want? Profit for its shareholders. Stability for its workforce. Growth.

Progressive corporations realize a healthier, happier, more energetic workforce will help it realize growth and profit faster. That's what we're selling: not massage, or fitness, or meditation: we're selling happy. We're providing an experience that can unite the staff, give them something in common outside work, and improve their productivity. We can reduce sick days (and we have the data to support the argument.) We can help them look better, feel better, and like their job better. In fact, most employees value "extra services" or "creative time" more than money, according to industry surveys.

The corporate market is slow moving but valuable. One corporate client could make a huge difference for a small-scale service firm, or add a degree of stability to a medium-sized firm. Some larger service providers can rely solely on the corporate market instead of trying to help one client at a time. But due to the bureaucratic nature of most large companies, it can take awhile to reach the right person. It can take even longer for a decision-maker to rule in your favor.

We start with a simple introduction (awareness stage.) This is usually in the form of a letter introducing our services (a copy is attached below.) We list the benefits of our service, not the features; and we provide 2-3 options for service.

Tactic: Workplace Seminars

The first option is, of course, to help for free. A free seminar on retirement savings plans, stretches to do at a desk or managing a budget provides the opportunity to move large groups into the "Desire" stage.

There are two goals of a seminar in a corporate environment:

1) Clearly demonstrate the benefits of your service;

2) Capture the contact information from everyone in attendance.

For example, if your firm provides tax advice for working professionals, hosting a seminar for upper-management employees will help them avoid over-taxation. It will create a benefit for the employer (grateful employees,) and introduce you to high-earning potential clients. It will establish your authority on the subject. Sharing some example scenarios—stories—instead of equations and vague tax laws will make your message stick. Offering to send everyone a free "tax-time checklist" will earn their trust (and email address.) Continue the conversation from that point of trust: send monthly high-value tips and reminders to save their receipts. Then, in March, invite them to bring their receipts to you and have their taxes prepared early.

If your service is fitness, a quick talk on nutrition and exercise can be followed by a very productive Q+A. Over the years, I've put more emphasis on the Q+A period, rather than dumping too much information and boring the audience early. Then a draw for some free PT sessions, or entry into a 30-day challenge, will capture email addresses for follow-up later.

Tactic: "Team-Building" Experiences

One of the largest target markets for Obstacle Course Races (like Spartan Race and Tough Mudder) is corporate teams. Surprised?

I was a kid when "corporate team-building" became vogue. My mother—a consultant for school boards—put on "workshops" to develop "mission statements" and such in the early 90s. But soon the concept moved out of the workplace and onto ropes courses, private islands and--well, cow pastures.

Team building can revolve around motivation, but also around relaxation or even mindfulness. Anything that requires a shared experience carries benefit to the corporation. For example, a full day of mindfulness, yoga and massage could help stressed-out managers return to a more productive state. On the other end of the spectrum, a physical challenge to elevate stress levels can create a feeling of "army buddies" and "survivorship." Where "trust falls" and Tony Robbins seminars used to be popular, many offices now sign up for Warrior Dashes or marathon relays. There's a huge opportunity here: helping the team prepare its fitness, or providing massage after the race, or preparing their nutrition before a group vacation will greatly enhance their experience. My friend Rich Borgatti fills this role for corporate groups preparing for Spartan Races. He runs training groups to reduce the risk of injury and build "obstacle immunity." After all, the point of the challenge is to find success as a group, not to find "failure" in a muddy field or lose productive workers to injury.

Tactic: 30-Day Challenges

Businesses can also build camaraderie through a drawn-out shared experience. If the team is working toward a common goal, they'll learn how to lean on each other for support. For example, a nutritionist could host a 30-day healthy eating challenge. The challenge could include an introductory seminar, a private Facebook group for all participants (see: "building an audience,") a downloadable tracking guide (to save printing fees and gain email accounts) and a prize for services at the end of the month.

Prizes can be donated by other service providers, like personal trainers or dress shops, but should also include consulting by the nutritionist as a "grand prize."

When the month is over, the nutritionist could address the private group: "Great job, everyone! Samantha won, but you all did really well! The next step is to book a private consultation with me (here's the link!) Who's ready for the next step?"

If clients move toward the private service (Integration phase,) great. If not, the audience can be kept in their seats for the next performance:

"For those who didn't sign up for one-on-one attention, that's okay: I'd like you to try this on your own for a month. I'll check in after 30 days to see how you're all doing."

30 days later, the nutritionist rejoins the group of dieters. If they're doing well, she congratulates them with, "Awesome job! Now who's ready to take the next step?" If, predictably, they've fallen off without her guidance, she can offer to help even more:

"That's okay, guys. We all need coaching. Who's ready to get some one-on-one help?"

30-day challenges can feature savings plans or pushups, meditation or tooth whitening. They're valuable, fun and effective for building teams. And they're usually not free: while they might not command more than $50 per participant, the value to the company will far exceed the price.

Tactic: Private Service

The overall goal of a corporate program is to draw a large number of clients to your service at once. Be careful to remember the value you're selling: a healthier, happier, more productive workforce. It might be tempting to offer discounts, but that's not a primary motivator for the decision-maker in the company. After all, it's not their money.

A subscription-based private service, covered by the company, is the golden standard. Some larger corporations (like Samsung) have incorporated CrossFit gyms into their factories. Other businesses, like Google, hire massage therapists to help their staff on Fridays. This creates a recurring and predictable revenue stream for the service provider.

My plumber doesn't take calls on the weekends (except for me, of course.) He goes fishing, because he has one large corporate contract. In slow months, he still has a predictable revenue stream from this client. In busy months, he services the corporate client first. Instead of hustling for each job individually, he charges a retainer.

A caterer could provide a similar service for a corporation. For example, the caterer could partner with the nutritionist in the above challenge, or offer lunchtime delivery for corporations who enroll a minimum number of employees in their meals-on-wheels program. Gyms can offer private groups to companies, too.

In 2007, I was approached by a local insurance company to do a free seminar for their staff. I took it a step further, and did a free bootcamp-style workout in their parking lot. The company paid for an 8-week private bootcamp; then the employees paid for another 8 weeks. It sold out again and again. Eight YEARS later, the group STILL show up at 8pm every Tuesday night for "sweat factory class." Most are gym members on top of the private group.

Tactic: Health and Wellness Days

Another option is to book a booth at the company's annual "Health Fair." Many hospitals, for instance, hold "Wellness Fairs" and invite multiple service providers to set up a booth. Nurses (like teachers) are a strong target market, because they have overlapping occupational and social bubbles: nurses tend to hang out with other nurses outside work. The goal of a health fair isn't to convince a passerby to sign up for your service. The goal is to establish awareness and continue the conversation later (moving them to the "Desire" stage.) Offer a draw for a free dress fitting or hairdo; collect names and email addresses, and announce a winner via email the next day. Offer everyone else an incentive to try your service (with a deadline.) For example: "Tammy Smith won the $200 makeover package. Congrats, Tammy! For everyone else, we want to thank you for your dedicated and thankless service. Nurses' Week is next week at Total Body Spa: bring in this coupon and get a free manicure with your wax!"

Sometimes the easiest way to get action from someone is to thank her in advance.

In "Mavens Strategy," I wrote about ways to start the conversation for your Mavens. These always included an offer to help a person in the Maven's social circles. But what if the maven's husband doesn't KNOW they need you? What happens when they think, "I'm doing just fine on my own, thanks!" What happens when they're scared?

You let them try your service WITH their spouse, or their friend. You show them how much they'll benefit from your service. And you tweak that service to a two-on-one.

The "Thank Up" requires the use of a gift card or "thank you" note. The note should double as an invitation: bring your spouse, and let's all do this together. I'll share my time to make it easy for them. We'll gang up on them, and when they're done, they'll share what we share.

The conversation goes like this:

"Bill, I've been trying to find a way to say

'thanks' for being such a great client. I know your wife is a bit nervous about trying my group classes, and that's okay. I'd like to invite her to try a two-on-one training session. It will be you, me and her together for a half hour. We'll do an easy little workout, and you can hold her hand the entire time. What do you think?"

On the card, you'll add an expiry date simply to create a sense of urgency. When Bill's wife Martha books their two-on-one session, you'll teach her to squat, and work to improve HIS squat. Then he'll do Tabata squats, and Martha will do 5 squats every 20 seconds, and they'll share something. You'll ask, "Martha, would you be more comfortable working out this way for awhile?" and then book the next session (not free.)

Another way to approach the "thank up" is to thank a non-client for their help.

"Martha, I know it must be tough to wrangle these three kids all the time, and we love having them here at the Gymnastics club. I also do some personal training here during the day, and I'd like to give you three free sessions as a "thanks for all you do." Can you come in on Monday for the first workout?"

In my case, we use a card with one of our branding hashtags on the front: #igotthis appears often in Catalyst social media. The card looks like this:

…and the back looks like this:

Now Y↑U
can, too!

**This card is worth a
FREE 30-minute personal training session
at Catalyst with ME and a coach.**

I love it there, and you will too. Promise.

Let's book before _____!"

705.256.1344 | CatalystGym.com | info@catalystgym.com

(note the expiry date.)

And the "thank up" goes exactly as I've written above. It's a great way to get a high-value client who might otherwise not consider our group fitness program. We look for opportunities to "thank up" our clients, and generally use the strategy two or three times each month.

Strategy: Maven Connections

"Mavens" are more than talkers. They're the up-in-your-business pest who won't leave you alone until you try…this. With them. Because they love it.

Mavens are usually women; almost always independent, Type-A spirits. They explore, find things they like, and go back for friends.

Your business probably has several Mavens: raving fans who drag their friends to your doorstep. But what about the other fans: those who love your service, but aren't great at talking about it? They can answer questions, but they're not salespeople; they won't wear a sandwich board up and down the street outside your door. It's our job to start the conversation for them, and that conversation begins with, "How can I help?"

As I wrote earlier, we all influence three groups: the people we live with; the people we work with; and the people with whom we have a "third place" in common.

Each month, choose three Mavens.

Solicit their story: what brought them to your door? What was their first impression? Why do they keep coming back? What's their favorite memory of your service? Use an emailed "interview" or a video.

Next, consider the social connections of each. Who do they live with? Who do they work with? With whom do they play golf / go to church / go to school / practice the clarinet? How can you help THOSE people?

Start the conversation with a "thanks": "Margaret, we love having you here. As a 'thank you,' I'd like to help brighten up your office with a free team-building workout at my gym. Who should I call to put this together?"

In the Brand Action chart, record one connection for each maven (or more, if the connection needs your help in an obvious way.) Stick with the low-hanging fruit. Make your approach, and track the results.

Pop quiz: a few hundred pages earlier, I gave two "Mavens" stories as examples. One was from my gym; another was a story I made up about a bookkeeper named Bryan.

At the end of the second story, the imaginary "maven" raved that she was terrified during an audit, but actually got a refund of....how much?

Most readers will remember: it was eight hundred dollars. THAT's the power of telling stories instead of sharing "testimonials": your brain is hard-wired to remember stories.

Strategy: Service Industry Referrals (Cobranding)

Your clients use the services of other professionals. Some of their clients will want to use your services, too.

In many cases, your services complement the service of others (a new suit looks better with a new haircut.) In the "Cobranding" section, I outlined a three-stage process for helping other business owners:

1. Give them gift certificates. Let them reward their clients with your service.
2. Invite the business owner to try your service (they're the "sneezers.")
3. Send your best clients to them, using their gift certificates as rewards.

It's a simple process, especially when you start with the clients already under your care.

In the "Establishing Authority" section of this book, I went into great depth on the value of content marketing. In the new economy, trust isn't built on familiarity, but open sharing of expertise. We no longer know the shoemaker; but we can still love the shoes.

Aim to publish three pieces of content each month. Be as diverse as possible: mix elements of long-form writing, short blog posts, social media, podcasts, photography and video. This is a major stumbling block for many; unfamiliar with media creation and editing, some small business owners will simply create a marketing blind spot around content creation.

It happens often, and here's my solution: use a clock.

Tactic: Use A Clock

One Thursday afternoon, after another conversation with a consulting client who was struggling to publish content, I decided to publish my OWN content to demonstrate how easy it really was.

I snagged two of my coaches, handed one my phone, and gave them these instructions:

"Go into the gym. Set the clock for precisely 60 minutes. Shoot as many exercise demo videos as possible in 60 minutes. Go."

They shot ten.

I took the memory card and edited the videos; that took 90 minutes. But in 2.5 hours, we'd created enough video to last me all Spring.

Tactic: On The Spot

In IgniteGym, we have clients practice public speaking by having them talk about random nouns for set intervals. For example, a client might stand with their back to a clock, and I'll say, "Brick."

The client will have to talk about bricks nonstop until time expires. More advanced clients can last for three or four minutes; beginners try to last for 20 seconds.

Service professionals ARE experts. When asked a direction question by a client, they can speak passionately and with authority. If all

else fails, have a client or coworker ask you a question while recording you on their phone.
Examples:

"Show me how to deadlift."

"Why should men use mousse instead of gel?"

"Why shouldn't people use low-carb diets?"

In my case, after much practice, I can last almost an hour if the topic is right.

You'll get better with practice, I promise. Start building momentum with clocks.

Strategy: Newsletters

Earlier in this book, I broke down the timing and template of the perfect newsletter. I recommended splitting recipients up by desire (what do they want?) and addressing their goals as directly as possible.
I also revealed the ideal layout for newsletters. But as with any content, a newsletter must be reliable and consistent. Clients must know to expect it around the same time every month.

Done well, they'll look for it; done poorly, they'll hit "spam" and become unreachable.

A good newsletter requires about an hour every month. It's worth it. To motivate myself, I track the number of "click-throughs" resulting in sales. My average newsletter is worth $400-$800 within the first two hours of publication. That's a great use of my time.

Strategy: Bring-A-Buddy

Sometimes the best invitation is an invitation. Hosting a special event—even one day each month—and urging clients to "bring a friend" can help create a sense of urgency.

For example, "buddy workouts" are more fun with a partner. If they're simple enough, a beginner can join.

Partner massages are also popular. Teaching a husband how to knead out his wife's exercise-related soreness is of great benefit to everyone.

"Bring-a-friend Friday" might look different to everyone. What if a dress shop held "private shows" for up to ten friends of the bride?

In a section called "Thank Up," I outlined a process for encouraging nervous clients to try your service by giving them an excuse to visit. This is popular in gyms, but could easily be effective in any service.

Fashion shows encourage buddy-recruitment. Ladies' Nights at garages make it easy for women to learn about cars in a less-intimidating environment (for some.) "Toy Hacks" can encourage new kids to visit a library. The key—as always—is to know what a target market WANTS. Is it a hand to hold? Is it novelty? Is it FUN?

When you place yourself in a client's shoes and dare to ask, "What do I want?" you're likely to figure it out. When you do, you'll be the most expert marketer on the planet. You'll find financial success. And you won't have to sell a thing.

Conclusions: Help First—AND Last

What Do I Want?

This is a funny question on which to rest my case, isn't it? After all, who CARES what I want?

Because I care what YOU want. And the best way to help you get what you want is to show you how to give others what THEY want.

Isn't that funny? You make them happy, and you get happy. I make you happy, and I get happy.

This, I tell my kids, is the secret: make people happy. Call it karma, or "paying it forward," or "The Secret" or exposing yourself to the universe. Call it whatever you want, just help others.

That's what I want.
Teach a man to fish. Help first. Then accept his invitation to dinner.

P.S.

While this book was in the editing process, I had the opportunity to share ten examples of the "Help First" philosophy with a group of 7,000 other service professionals.
Overnight, I gained 100 Facebook "friends." I don't believe most were inspired by the actual strategies, but the stories. If you take nothing else from this book, take this: tell the stories of your clients. Brag them up. Put them first. Help them find their podium.

#1: Guys, I'm lucky: I get inspired every day by some of the best gyms in the world. And I preach that winning isn't the result of motivation; that motivation is the result of winning. So for the next 10 days, I'm going to share one big "win" with you every day.
These are examples of how to practice the "Help First" way; to help more people without resorting to sales "techniques," discounts, ads, or overcoming objections (you won't have any.) Hopefully, you can use these to build your OWN momentum. First, meet C and T. I met C when his daughter joined our CFK program, and offered to help him. He brought his wife, who was nervous about CrossFit, so I asked if they'd prefer to train together. They chose PT over group, and immediately became a $10,000 annual client. No sales pitch, no discount, just an offer to help. When their son was cut from his hockey team, I offered to help. He eventually gave up hockey to join his sister in CFK. No pitch, just "I think I can help." Then I asked how I could help their daughter gain

work experience. She quickly became a peer mentor for to help IgniteGym kids integrate into CFK. Inspired, C and T committed to donating 5% of every sale at any three of their hardware stores from any Catalyst client to the Ignite program. As a "thank you," I invited their staff in for a fun workout. We had a fun team-building experience. No specials, no discounts, no set of steak knives. See you tomorrow!

#2: Every month, we approach three local corporations and offer a free seminar for their staff. In September, this led to a proposal for a huge deal: 50 staff for 3x/week for 3 months. We were underbid, but the HR director liked us better, and offered us a chance to provide the service at a significant discount.
I said no, turning down a huge gross return, because the net wasn't worthwhile. They gave the contract to someone willing to work for $25/hr. I offered to give them a free seminar anyway. Last week, the HR director called. She's with a new company, and felt we were the only "professional" coaching around. We'll set up a team-building workout in September. But for now, she signed up with her husband for 2-on-1 training. I don't have a photo yet, but hopefully this story paints a picture of how "Help First" works: I offered help in the "Awareness" stage, and led them to "desire." Integration took awhile, but didn't include discounts or "specials"--and that led them to a much larger purchase later. And retention is

our strength; you'll see them holding little "PR" whiteboards on my page soon.

#3: Yesterday, my daughter took a skating lesson from a former NHL pro. He's newly retired, and looking to build a business around hockey coaching.
After the lesson, I thanked him and asked how I could help him build his business. He mentioned that he was looking for goalies for his skaters to shoot on. I have several goalies in our CFK program, so I emailed them and asked if they'd like some free ice time. They were pumped.
Next, I offered him a free concussion seminar for parents while their kids skated with him. I gave him a link to my nutrition strategy guide (a landing page) and he promised to send it to all his skaters. He asked, "What can I do to help YOU now?" That was an easy one: skate with my Ignite clients. I told him I'd pay for ice rental and find helmets and skates for 100 kids if he'd grab a few buddies and skate with our kids at Christmas. We shook on it. Two hours later, a semipro player walked into our gym, sent by the same coach. "He told me to quit [X gym] and start here today."

#4: Guys, meet L. He started at my gym on Wednesday.
L has some anxiety and depression issues. He's only 17. His home life sucks. But he doesn't need Prozac. He doesn't need to talk about his feelings. He needs a WIN.
This is a 550lb tire.
A social agency was thrilled to buy him 20 1:1

sessions (>$1000)after he flipped that tire. He left here with a purpose and a massive bright spot that became my own.
Ask, "Who needs my help?" Then, "How can I help them?"

#5: This is a camera crew.
A few weeks ago, one of our members was promoting a charity 5k. We called the local TV station on her behalf; she asked to film the spot in our box.
While they were here, they mentioned that most businesses call them for self-promotion; we called them to help someone else. I asked if they'd like to try a workout in private, and the cameraman agreed.
As I write this, two cameramen are doing OnRamp Day 2--on camera. We're doing a series of movement demos to help local viewers get started with their fitness. It's a 10-part series. Oh, and those are some
logs "Help First" includes the members you already have. How can you help them, their spouses, their coworkers and their friends?
 When you look for opportunities to HELP instead of to SELL, you'll find them everywhere. I posted 5 from my own gym this week, but there have been more...

#6: R has been doing CrossFit for three years. She's visiting my city for a month, and then returning to her regular box. Since she's here for so long, we asked to chat with her before she started training (our "No Sweat" consultation.)
After listening to her for ten minutes, we knew

one-on-one training was better for her than group. She faced a number of plateaus, and agreed the month was a great time to focus on those things before returning to group. She signed up for a 1:1 package that was 3x her normal "unlimited" rate.

I asked if her gym--which is usually running some sort of discount, "promo" or deal-- provided 1-on-1 services. She said no. "They've never offered it," she said. "But to be fair, I don't think I've ever had a 20-minute conversation with the coaches there."

#7: Guys, meet W. I met him at a cancer benefit. The booth beside mine was selling 10 sessions of Personal Training for $99. I was just there to talk.

W talked for over thirty minutes about his wife's health problems. He showed up at my gym the next Monday to start training.

That was 13 years ago.

W pays a bit more for private attention. "Those CrossFit guys are nuts," he says. Then: "What's the name of this WOD again?" When I make business decisions, these are the clients I think about first. How will this new policy affect me in 20 years? How will this pricing structure set up my business for the long haul? Would I want my kid to take over my business in the shape it's in? When I retired from PT a few years ago, W moved to another Catalyst coach without missing a single session. He saw the long-term plan because we spoke about it often. Outside the gym, he's watching his friends slide down that gray slope and says, "That's not gonna be me." There are many lessons to be learned from W (and the others who have passed the 10-year mark at Catalyst) but I'll stop there. (To answer questions in advance: the other gym is bankrupt. And W's wife still hasn't started.)

#8: Last December, I was invited to speak at a local business about "new trends in fitness and health." During the Q+A, one of the attendees asked, "I saw you behind the bench at a hockey game last weekend. Your kids had a ton of energy at 7am! They steamrolled our kids. How did you get them to do that?" I said, "I told their parents what to feed them before the game. I can write it down for you if you like." Hands shot up all over the room, and I collected their email addresses. I posted, "How To Feed A Hockey Animal" (http://catalystgym.com/feed-hockey-animal/) on our site and sent out the link. I boosted the post for $6 for one day, and had 56 parents sign up for our Catalyst Varsity newsletter. Within a month, our kids' groups had a waiting list. We opened more groups and filled them too. Every month, I send them articles from CFJ or other sources. Sometimes I talk about the value of public speaking for kids and other non-fitness topics. In June, we launched "Varsity Sport" for kids who wanted even more. They train at a higher level for CFK competitions, but can also choose to assist with our jammed Kids' classes, or even be paid to help integrate Ignite kids into CFK. In September, some will start earning money by tutoring younger kids. And there's still a waiting list, thanks to a 6-level retention system allowing kids to graduate up. The coach of our Varsity programs is paid on the 4/9 model, and makes more per month from Varsity alone than most other coaches I've met. That growth started from a simple offer to help: I had information that would help someone else, and I shared it. You probably already have the information that will help your next client...

#9: This is Tyler.
A few years ago, Ty was an elementary school teacher. But he thought he could do better than the curriculum he was being forced to teach. He went through our Internship program to coach, but wanted to do more. I created an opportunity through the "intrapreneurship" concept outlined in my books. IgniteGym eventually became its own company, but started as a specialty program built on the 4/9 payment model.
But this post isn't about Ignite.
This post is about a quote from Coach at the last Affiliate Gathering: "The best gyms create meaningful career opportunities for their coaches." I like owning multiple companies. But I LOVE giving game-changers like Ty the opportunity to build a business to support his family. I love moving guys like Ty toward wealth: a high value for their time and passion. And all my coaches are given the same help when they identify a particular passion or niche. I own other businesses, but the "Help First" model is the same. When they succeed, I do too.

#11: Also pictured is S, a personal hero.

He's been doing CrossFit and Ignite for about a year and a half. He was completely nonverbal when he started, and spent the first six months at the gym just running laps. I was seriously concerned that his parents wouldn't continue the service as he didn't seem to be making much progress.

Then his older sister showed up at a "bring-a-buddy" workout. When I shook her hand, she said: "Oh, YOU'RE Christmas!"

Obviously, I was confused.

"Christmas?" I asked.

"Yeah, S talks about you at home. He says 'go to gym. Ty and Christmas.'"

Well, I...

To see a video of S saying "Good Morning!" at the gym, visit facebook.com/IgniteGym.

They help me as much as I help them.

Made in the USA
Columbia, SC
26 May 2018